Beyond My Manor

Beyond My Manor

A Life of My Choosing -
Not Giving a Fig, Is Not the Best Option!

FAIZI O. HASHMI

PARTRIDGE
A Penguin Random House Company

ISBN: Hardcover   978-1-4828-4823-6
            Softcover   978-1-4828-4824-3
            eBook   978-1-4828-4822-9

Print information available on the last page.

To order additional copies of this book, contact
Partridge India
A PENGUIN RANDOM HOUSE COMPANY
1663 Liberty Drive
Bloomington, IN 47403
000 800 10062 62
orders.india@partridgepublishing.com

www.partridgepublishing.com/india

CONTENTS

For Sadaf, Aatif, Yasmin
who are the cause of my happiness

For Baji, Abbu, Ammi, Abbi
whose blessings are eternal

For Sanjeev, Sarvesh, Ashwani. Guljit
who give stimulus to my thinking

And in fond memories of:

RazmiRizwan Husain
Amitabh Bhattacharya
Mohun Kudesia

*"Yesterday I was clever, so I wanted to change the world.
Today I am wise, so I am changing myself" – Rumi*

FOREWORD

It is with great pleasure that I write these words for Faizi Hashmi, my student at JNU quite some decades ago. Even as a student, Faizi's interests were wide ranging, far beyond the confines of medieval history in which he had enrolled for specialization. After excelling in his Master's and M.Phil., Faizi decided to opt for administrative services, which was a loss to academia. I have not kept pace with his administrative career, but the collection of his writings in this volume attests his attention to, indeed his passion for the issues that concern him and concern us all. Issues that encompass a huge range from the absence of civility in daily life to the destruction of ecology, from celebrating the great cultural plurality of India now under increasing threat to the construction of competitive nationalisms, from showering reverence at great icons like Swami Vivekanand and Atal Bihari Vajpeyi to Nani Palkhivala, not merely at the Mahatma and Jawaharlal Nehru, to feeling pain at the neglect of the unsung heroes and of other icons like the great rivers of India. The very fact that he was constantly keeping up his reading and was committing his concerns to writing and publishing in columns underscores his caliber as an out of the ordinary bureaucrats.

Faizi's writings are not merely an exercise of the mind, but ones imbued with solutions to problems we face as individuals and as a collective. He has both learnt greatly from life as a citizen and as an administrator and given serious thought to these before writing them down. Agreement with him is not a condition of appreciating these. It is a collection worth waiting for, for its lucidity and its ability to leave us questioning a bit of ourselves.

Harbans Mukhia
Retired Professor of History and Rector
Jawaharlal University
New Delhi

PREFACE

It would be preposterous to claim any divine ordainment for writing a book; much less any altruistic motivations. It started for purely practical reasons derived from the learning that some of the good deeds return; further the belief that most humans somehow or the other touch the lives of others. If that touch is positive, its cumulative effect on the lives of fellow men and women may be stupendous. So I thought, why not remind myself of this? Besides, there is the imperative of speaking up or standing up. The Chain of Change has to begin at some point – so the words of exhortation. Sharing the thoughts with the world at large was therefore the next logical step ahead.

Working in the government not only means several and on occasions onerous responsibilities but also certain imposed restrictions and rule-bound limitations on freedom of action. Luckily non-political writing and non-critical references to government or its policies are exempted. Thus this permissible activity I could rely upon to make some constructive propositions in a societal framework. But the views expressed in these pages are personal to me and no way reflect on the thinking of the government.

Many of these write-ups have appeared in newspapers and magazines during the last couple of years. Why a book now? Magazines and newspapers by their very design have a short shelf-life, besides lacking in documentation value and spread. The reach of their contents also gets limited by the fact that the papers are often not read in their entirety. Readers sometimes miss some columns as one hears frequently from family and friends. This gap is likely to be met by a book in a substantive way. With passage of time, some of these articles also needed to be revisited and updated, which has been possible through this edition.

We all guard our freedom very jealously; our private space is considered inviolable. But are we not taking our liberties for granted? Freedom to do what – to remain silent, do nothing! Freedom has to be to give life – a meaning and purpose, fulfillment and growth, health and happiness, peace and harmony, decency and dignity, education, recreation and leisure, freedom from poverty and diseases, from dirt and filth, from inequality, discrimination and injustices, in totality to touch the lives of others in a giving and caring way and thereby improve the quality of life. We have to look beyond ourselves if we want a better world for our children.

We cannot miss the glaring civic deficiencies that affect the Quality of Life in our cities. Non-adherence to basic civic laws means that there is not only disregard for the law of the land but also that we have a rather low 'Citizenship Quotient', resulting from negligence of value education and lack of training through citizenship awareness programs. It has to be built through participation and involvement amongst the citizenry. Unless the communities come together, get organized, stand for social causes and build networks, we will not develop, what came to be described as the 'Social Capital'. The concept was perhaps earliest implied in the writings of Alexis de Tocqueville, later expounded by scholars like James Coleman, Pierre Bourdieu, and very adroitly by Robert Putnam in his *'Bowling Alone: America's Declining Social Capital'*. We may add to this the 'Quality of Life' elucidated by Robert Costanza and others, including the World Bank. This socio-cultural rejuvenation, along with the creation of wealth – not the subject of this book, we may agree, builds Reputation of an Urban Conglomerate and give it the competitive advantage. Should that not be our national objective?

I have created a blog by the same name, and could not decide on anything better than the name as 'Beyond My Manor' for this book. The chapters are not meant to create any artificial barriers; some pieces of two different chapters may be organically linked or may have close connections. But I considered making some intelligible differentia as necessary and helpful for focused reading.

I shall be happy to receive feedback from the readers about the subjects discussed. Comments and suggestions are accordingly welcome for my continued education and shall be graciously acknowledged.

ACKNOWLEDGEMENT

I believe that no task, big or small can ever be accomplished by one person and one has to be ever grateful to various people for their support, encouragement and contribution. This small endeavor has been made possible with the help of family, friends and well-wishers. I would have liked to thank them all individually but that turns out to be difficult on account of constraint of space.

My first writings started appearing on a web portal, Merinews and I therefore owe them sweet thanks. I started writing regularly in Pioneer (Dehradun and Chandigarh editions) some years ago after Siddhart Mishra introduced me to his team. I am thankful to them. My friend, Sakina introduced me to the 'Speaking Tree' of the Times of India that gave me an opportunity to write on spiritual matter. Some of the articles included in this book in their pre-revised version appeared in two magazines, 'Bureaucracy Today' and 'Governance Now'. I am thankful to these Publications and their editors for this, and for their support to me to rely upon my columns for further use.

I was encouraged to write by my dear friend, Sanjeev Chopra who has been like a philosopher friend and I endearingly acknowledge his encouragement and support. I learnt a lot through discussions with close friends and thank them all very sincerely - Guljit, Ashwani, Askari, Sarvesh, Suhaib, Ajai, Meenu, Sakina and Farhan. I also thank my other friends and well-wishers who have in their own ways contributed to my awakening.

A man is a product of his environment. My gratitude is therefore due to my alma mater, AMU and JNU which during my formative years inculcated in me the spirit of inquiry and discussion, and encouraged me to question moribund beliefs and practices through a vibrant culture of openness and debate. I was lucky to be taught by eminent historians at these two Universities. My training through PGPPM at IIMB helped me to adept to rigours of research and subjecting postulates to validation. The same needs to be mentioned about Maxwell School of Public Policy, University of Syracuse, USA and KDI, Seoul, South Korea, wherein training programs were scholastic and insightful. I owe gratitude to these institutions.

As his student, I always held Prof. Harbans Mukhia of JNU in great esteem and received his love and affection. I didn't know then that one day he would write the Foreword of my first book. He is an erudite scholar and a great teacher of medieval Indian history. It is my good fortune that my book is being introduced to the audience by a scholar of his eminence and repute.

My friend, Prof. Farhan Ahmad Nizami, Director, Centre of Islamic Studies, Oxford University is a highly respected and globally known historian. His writing of the Afterword of my book is of great significance for me and a matter of immense personal satisfaction. I am thankful to both these gentleman, one my teacher and another my friend.

Partridge India has been my valued collaborator for the publication of this book. While the Company turned out to be responsive and responsible, it were her Associates who professionally interacted with me from the day one. I am thankful to each member of the Team Partridge. I would also like to thank Chandan, Brajesh, Ruchi and Lalit for their time.

My father *(Abbu)*, though a legal luminary is also an erudite scholar of literature. His lessons to me from childhood have stayed with me and enkindled in me a love for literature. My late beloved mother was a great source of inspiration for me. She always encouraged me to go for higher education. I am sure she would be smiling from wherever she is. Wish she was around to see her 'moon' as a writer. God bless her soul! I miss you *Baji*.

It has been the dream of my wife to see my book published. She endured not only long hours whilst I spent my time away from her but also encouraged, sweet-talked and guided me; suggested themes and treatment of subjects on several occasions. She truly has been a friend philosopher guide to me – thanks Yasmin for being there. Both my children, Sadaf and Aatif have been most endearingly supporting and reassuring always. Many times they came up with subjects to be commented upon and even did some research for me including fixing my photographs and proof reading of my manuscript. I am deeply indebted to my family for their love and affection without which this work would not have seen the light of the day.

TO LIVE AND LET LIVE

TO LIVE AND LET LIVE

A Chain for Change could be a Good Idea

Bystanders are people who remain silent spectators even while witnessing some blatant wrong happening before their eyes. It is in that context that the new Hindi film 'Jai Ho' has come out with an interesting response. The hero of the film frequently gets into fights for protecting the rights of others. But he does not accept a 'thank you' from anyone he helps. Instead he asks his legatee to help three others, with further request to each three of them to convey the same message to those they go on to help and so forth. He envisages, though without saying so in words, that this will keep multiplying and a chain of do-gooders will be created in due course. The new device starts spreading through word of mouth and even the Chief Minister of the State gets interested to know as to who started the chain.

Films are thoroughly fictionalized and present a make believe world, quite often just in two shades of black and white. Despite that limitation the concept depicted in the film is fresh and should encourage and motivate the altruists further. The stand taken by Salman Khan, the main protagonist in the film that even one person can make a difference has an appeal and is presented in a disarmingly convincing way. Since we were told right from our young age to pick good beliefs and principles from wherever one got, this good motto depicted in the film may be picked up by one and all and spread over by word of mouth. Even if a small percentage of those who initially agree to help three persons, actually do so, a chain of change will start emerging in the way we conduct ourselves with respect to other human beings, whether related or perfect strangers. The axiom as highlighted in the film of helping three people and asking them to convey the same message to those, whom they help, may start the process of levitation of the collective social conscience of the society to a higher level. This would not only help in protecting the dignity, life and property of many people, it will promote general goodness and engender happiness.

Many of the woes in the urban social landscape today result from lack of civility, care and concern. Helping somebody in need is like giving (in charity), and giving definitely provides as much happiness to the giver as to the recipient. That apart, extending a helping hand to a person in distress or for that matter, even speaking up against a wrong, would be a great contributor to social well-being. So if not effective intervention, at least raising a voice that is audible enough against a wrong would herald the reversal of the ill effects of silence.

The political scenario in the country is passing through a massive churning today. The issues like hearing the voice of the people, empathy with their trials and tribulations, injustices of the system, hardships and deprivations faced by the masses are all being underlined like never before. As awareness about rights and entitlements rise, so also the aspiration to be heard, and a more vocal affirmation that injustice is no longer acceptable. The recent spate of mass participation of people in and protests on public issues for good governance, for transparency and efficiency has led to intense discussion on rights and wrongs and the accountability of the government decisions. In a way, the population is today more receptive to social ideals, but these would have an edge if coming from credible social and political leaders. Be that as it may, the country is perhaps moving towards and warming up to adopt new ideas for bringing a change for the better.

Coming to the aid of a person in need of help is acknowledged as a noble deed in all religions. It is also said in our culture that good deed revisits the doer with more goodness. It does not matter if one is not a believer and refuses to accept the sayings from divine scriptures. But she may perhaps still agree that the godless cosmos also has some scheme woven around the celestial objects – reflected from their remarkable equilibrium and rhythmic movements – as much as around the lives of living beings and because they interact with and impact each other, so as to maintain a balance, it necessarily ordains some kind of mutual dependence. When there is mutual dependence, can 'help' be far behind?

The non-religious contextual framework is therefore also available that throws up the need to stand up and be counted against a wrong. However, it is a challenge to realize the ethical standard or positive human emotion. A wide audience of the citizenry may be targeted to make them willing participants of the process of social reengineering whereby the act of extending help is internalized. This would be like giving a rejuvenating stimulus to the people to think beyond their own selves. Though 'catch them young' is a better prescription and more result-oriented, 'better late than never' is worth applying for holding 'adult education program' – for bringing about an attitudinal change. Since even one person can make a difference, let us without waiting for a messiah, make a small beginning and take tentative steps towards that objective.

A Clean Street in Goa

Intervene for a Better World

Hugo Maurice Julian Claus noted Belgian author, poet, playwright, painter and film director said, *"I am a person who is unhappy with things as they stand. We cannot accept the world as it is. Each day we should wake up foaming at the mouth because of the injustice of things"*. Viewed in this context, it may be noted that the incidents of urban day-time petty crimes in general, eve-teasing and molestation attempt on women, incidents of street violence and road rage, civic offences etc. may be genuinely expected to be lesser in number but for the lack of citizen involvement – just involvement, not suggesting a vigilante move. Looking from a different perspective than policing and law-enforcement - which constitute the most important aspect in crime prevention and control - raising the consciousness of the citizens through sustained education and creating an enabling atmosphere should be a good public policy for curbing a wrong or socially unaccepted behaviour in public view.

This participation becomes more important not only in the context of limitation of state intervention per se, but for the sheer impossibility of policing every nook and corner of the urban landscape or the burgeoning population. There are instances of citizen police etc. experimented in some metros, albeit with limited success. The idea being suggested here is different – it is about building the moral commitment and capacity of the citizenry to try and stop offences in public view. Lest we misunderstand, this is not calling for acts of vigilantes, who have over the years conveyed a negative image of themselves by taking the law into their own hands.

While trying to build a framework, an illustration is made out, which on the face of it may look little over-simplistic but may help nevertheless. Grave crimes against women for example, from wife bashing to bride burning to rape, are not likely to be committed in public places, at least during the day time because there are many people around. So apparently the presence of people becomes a deterrent against certain offences. If we analyze closely, it is not as much the presence of people that matters as the perceived assurance of intervention by those present around, on behalf of the victim to be, to deter the commission of the intended crime. How successful that presence becomes on several occasions may be a matter of statistics and debate. But perception does matter and plays an important role in crime prevention; potential offenders are often daunted by such perception, e.g. the concept of Broken Window Theory in policing terminology.

If this non-acceptance by the community of anti-social behaviour by cognition and a sense of social responsibility is expanded to include vandalism and rowdism, many likely offences may record a downward trend. Thus the idea is to try to reverse the silence of the majority to prevent violence by the few. The general trend in society of not intervening when petty offences take place in the markets, trains, buses, theatres, parks or any public place indirectly encourages commission of graver offences. The social apathy creates environment not conducive to safe living. The attitude of being a bystander or a mute witness is disturbing.

Martin Luther King Jr. said, *"Our lives begin to end the day we become silent about things that matter"*. There are studies to explain why bystanders remain silent or do not intervene while socially unacceptable things happen in front of their eyes. Perhaps, the bystander is not sure about the typology of the offence or his own role or waits to be guided by the response of 'others' in the crowd. He is conditioned by various factors, including up-bringing, education, felt need, protecting self from likely harm and most importantly the presence or absence of empathy in relation to strangers.

Since we now have some idea of attitude and positioning of persons in a given situation where intervention would have saved the life, property or honour of another person, we may look at factors that could promote favorable environment. The idea to help anybody in distress or in trouble has to be inculcated from the very beginning. Above all, the message should be that help has to extend not only to friends and family but even to strangers in difficulty. Thus, coming forward to the aid of victim of a crime or an injured person has to be a learnt convention of a citizen, acquired through basic education from an early age. It would have to be emphasized that ethically it is incumbent upon a citizen to intervene in such situation. It may be additionally stated that the persons before intervening may take stock of the situation and better solicit support of others present so as to secure himself before coming to the help of a person in need.

In India, we do not have civic laws – like in Quebec, Brazil and USA – mandating such initiatives by citizens and for protecting the interventionist from any harassment arising from such interventions. This becomes important in emergency situations where a human life can be saved through intervention of bystanders, especially during the golden hour. With legal protection, urban life may become safer as spirited persons may then come forward to help and not remain silent spectators. We may conclude by quoting Derrick A. Bell from his book, Ethical Ambition: Living a Life of Meaning and Worth, *"Courage is a decision you make to act in a way that works through your own fear for the greater good as opposed to pure self-interest. Courage means putting at risk your immediate self-interest for what you believe is right".*

Urban Etiquettes
- Civility, Care and Concern

We are dreaming of developing our cities as world class, the phrase is often used for our metros and is intended to explain attainment of urban infrastructures and services of such quality as would match international standards. While the physical attributes being talked about are worth attaining but far from realized, it is the intangibles that are grossly inadequate. It must be recognized that social grooming, developing a rounded personality and acquisition of soft skills are as important for individuals as for a cultural entity. Our cities are clearly wanting in these as reflected in the acts of citizenry. Road rage is an extreme example of that trait; everyday uncivil response of the citizens and the public display of rude attitude is a more commonplace instance. The fact that people in a given situation do not show care and concern for each other is too glaringly evident and has to be understood in a perspective. We should then try analyzing its symptoms along with some corrective suggestions.

What is apparent at the first glimpse is the 'elbow syndrome', an aggressive demeanor as the dominant attribute of citizens. Pushing one's way by hook or by crook without consideration for the other person is a practiced response for most. The tendency is to move ahead for seizing a place under the sun at whatever cost. If someone else suffers in the process, it is none of my business. Whether this is the general feature of a society that suffers from gross inequalities and economic deprivation or more precisely where people are still struggling for their bread and butter, is for the sociologists to answer. Apparently, limited opportunities and inadequate resources available for large numbers do perhaps play a role in intensifying the struggle for spoils and to that extent there is an inherent tendency to be pushy, callous and unmindful of others travail. But this explanation suffers from some flaw. It does not explain why a well-heeled person who must be considered more self-assured behaves the same way, perhaps worse and fails to show humility and politeness in social situations, even where his immediate gains are not under threat. So this has to do with attitude and therefore, a socio-cultural rather than an economic issue.

Let us look at some broad generalizations that we encounter in daily life to draw parallels for a better understanding. We come across statements like, "people in down south are very disciplined", "Punjabis are a very hard-working people", "Bengalis are an intelligent lot" etc. – these cannot be said to be proven assertions but only certain stereotypes. Similar generalizations prevail with reference to etiquette issue, i.e. uncivil behaviour is sought to be explained by citing poverty, lack of literacy etc. and therefore, not a big deal; as the society progresses and economy expands, manners would gradually be imbibed. It is submitted that it is a big deal indeed, especially in the context of Globalization and our much closer daily interaction with the outside world that brings embarrassment to Indians.

Everyday experience in the markets, at stations, in offices, in banks, in restaurants etc. leaves one with a bitter taste in the mouth – nobody would wait one moment for allowing the other to complete his transaction. Who likes to be pushed in a queue? Why could not we wait to enter a metro coach before first letting the passengers to alight or permitting the people to come out of a lift before barging in? The social intercourse has increasingly become discordant. Rudeness as exemplified by some of the popular TV serials has become meritorious. Impoliteness is in fashion and offensive behaviour in public is a glory. What happened to the *Lukhnavi* culture of *'pehleaap'*(you first)? A train would be missed even as a gentleman would offer to be aside, giving way to the other first. The suave *aap* has become a curt tuu (thou), and uttered in a brasher manner. While we may rejoice having buried that culture, people in many cities abroad are known for showing courtesies even to perfect strangers.

Lessons in politeness and good conduct are learnt early in life. These are part of overall social grooming that is imparted first at homes and then in schools. But we forget that not everybody takes the learning of schools and colleges home – some people have to be retold the lesson and reoriented. There is need for Behaviour Change Communication of a very high order. The prime task is to emphasize politeness as a virtue. Adherence to civic and traffic rules, showing respect for women, senior citizens, foreigners, fellow passengers, in short a general civil behaviour on the street. Unfortunately we are not law-abiding by nature – citizens have construed democracy as license, with no concomitant responsibility. All concern is about rights and entitlements but no worry about duties. This deficiency has to be pointed out and hammered repeatedly through school curriculum, public forums, academic institutions, social clubs, RWAs, MTAs etc. Small-family norms and universalization of school education gradually came to be adopted by even the lower middle classes on account of sustained media campaigns over the years. Promotion and enforcement of civility, care and concern as inherent qualities of a good citizen must likewise become the new age mantra. There is no short cut but the beginning of a sound policy is never too late.

The Pathology of Law-breaking

S wami Vivekananda, the great Indian philosopher sarcastically referred to adults devoid of civic values as 'moustached babies'. This showed how peeved he was at the attitude of our people, who did not exhibit expected norms of social behaviour. A great thinker that he was, he died at a comparatively younger age leaving so much treasure of thoughts for his countrymen – attacking age-old cultural taboos. Relating to irrationality in food habits, he referred to our obstinate reliance on these (then) as 'religion of kitchen'. There is no attempt at internalising such gems of wisdom. The best of the so-called elite sets no example to be emulated by the lesser mortals. It is interesting though that many of these persons start behaving once they set their foot on a foreign land for fear of being ridiculed.

A highly irresponsible public behaviour is urinating in public spaces. Khushwant Singh rightly called those urinating on the road sides as 'slaves of their bowels'. It is so disgusting to find people urinating on Delhi roads in broad day light after parking their cars or scooters. Who are these guys? They are not our poor slum dwellers without a shelter or access to basic amenities. They are typical middle and even upper classes that pride itself in everything but have no training in basic etiquettes. One needs to ask them why cannot they wait till they reach their place of work, residence or whatever their destination before deciding to make a public display of their prostatic impairment? These people are in need of help. How else could one explain such uncouth and nasty scenes enacted daily on city roads? So if some adults (not old, genuine sufferers) still need to wear their nappies, they can only be called moustached babies.

We are infested with littering bug. Go to any public park, monument, market, railway station, there will be heaps of garbage that you wonder if the municipal van has just unloaded itself. Fact is, in our total blindness to the surrounding, we revel in spreading filth – it is the duty of the municipal workers to clean the mess that is what they are here for – irrespective of our educational background, cast or creed. No place can ever be kept clean by some hired hands until the citizenry performs its basic duty to take care and make some contribution towards that objective. The littering habit shows that we are the 'moustached babies' as bemoaned by Swami Vivekananda, and have grown up without inculcating any of the adult learning.

Swami Vivekananda is not there to guide us. But why doesn't each one of us ask questions? When I see a person throwing an empty can or pet bottle from a moving sedan after lowering his power window, I wonder what would be his upbringing like or social background. How can a civilized person throw rubbish on the street? It is pathetic to find litters strewn all over the city spaces, streets, markets and parks despite the dust-bins placed in good number. This filth is spread by people who are all 'well-connected' and 'influential' people and not street urchins.

An interesting booklet by Swami Ranganathananda, 'Enlightened Citizenship and Our Democracy', being a compendium of his discourses given in a symposium in 1980, in a very simple and lucid language, explained his well-researched ideas on civic values in Indian context. Even three decades earlier, he was complaining about the absence of civic values, declining standards of urban living, and lack of community feelings. He characterized these negative traits in one phrase, the 'pathology of law-breaking'.

This expression very appropriately conveys the lack of civic virtues in citizens, and one could not agree more. How else would one explain people parking their car or bike and urinating on city streets in broad-day light, littering on the streets, jumping the traffic signal, blaring horns like mad and indulging in vandalism at heritage sites? These people are in need of help. They are 'moustached babies' of Vivekananda and suffer from 'pathology of law-breaking' of Ranganathananada.

Reflecting on the lack of responsible behaviour, Nani Palkhivala said, "While eternal vigilance is undoubtedly the price of liberty, yet in a more profound sense eternal responsibility is also part of the price of liberty". Responsibility (of thinking, conduct and behaviour) thus in a manner of speaking becomes the core of civic discipline. We may recall that some of these were sought to be ingrained by incorporation of Fundamental Duties in the Indian Constitution in 1976. Though law alone cannot bring about a change should be crystal clear to all; it is a behaviour change communication issue to be achieved through a mix of socially marketing the civic ideas and enforcing it through strict regulatory framework.

The need is to make a beginning somewhere. Our urban landscape is in desperate need of reinventing itself in terms of adherence to law and observance of basic norms of civic behaviour. The quality of life defines a place and that among other things depends on altering the undesirable behaviours enlisted above. When the debate is now centring on the image market, those cities would be more competitive whose inhabitants start living within the boundaries of law.

A Typically Filthy Street in a Western India Town

A Junkyard in the Heart of a North Indian City

Noise Pollution in Our Cities

An obnoxious attribute of Indian motorists is to keep blaring horn without any rhyme or reason. It gives them sadistic pleasure to scare away other motorists, who happen to be in front of their vehicle. Honking is considered an uncivil behaviour in most other countries. But we don't care. Our collective unconcern to this menace is most inexplicable. The vehicular noise causes annoyance and leads to nerve-wrecking stress in urban sprawls. We have not woken up to this hazard yet. Two aspects need elaboration. First, we are deficient in soft skills is well known – politeness and courtesies aren't really our forte – but violation of traffic rules falls in another domain, i.e. relating to lack of respect and fear of law. Secondly, a duty is cast upon the road users to observe the public health and safety norms, failing which they need to bear the cost.

The new government at the Centre has launched *Swaccha Bharat Abhiyan*(Clean India Campaign). This belated public policy prescription needs to be complimented by crusading against the other filth, namely, noise pollution. With hundreds of thousands of first-generation car owners, with two to three cars per family, and unrestricted bludgeoning number of all types of vehicles, and all of them happily blaring horns all the time, peace in cities is a mirage. Every nook and corner of our habitat is affected by vehicular noise, most of which is contributed by deafening horns. While the sound of machines is still bearable, it's impossible to tolerate the pain of honking.

Sometimes one wonders whether this habit of honking is related to 'obsessive compulsive disorder' or some pathological disorientation – clinical psychologist may give a better diagnosis. In any case, our motorists are definitely in the need of help and earlier the better for all of us. But could there be other reasons like lack of community-mindedness, or a failure to understand what constitutes civility or concern for the society in which one lives?

Or has it come around owing to lack of exposure at an early age to developing appropriate social skills within the family, a fault line in the school curriculum, which doesn't give such aspects more than a flitting ritualistic touch, lack of involvement in community affairs, an apathy to the world around us – an attitude that is the product of an 'elbow society' – enforcing and reinforcing the aggressive disposition of some individuals? Is it an 'acquired social deficiency syndrome' (ASDS), if such a term can be used? We have no answers but the affliction needs to be treated in the larger interest of the society.

That brings our discussion to the issue of lack of respect for the law and the role of law-enforcement agencies. We know that those who zip around in high speeds, commit road-rage offences, jump the red lights causing danger to the lives of others, blow horns in total disregard to the law and to the detriment of the public health have scant respect for the law and they do it with immunity because they know that there is no cost to such juvenile behaviour. Mildly put, some motorists may lack awareness of this public health hazard. So they need to be exposed to the perils of noise pollution and given appropriate class room training. Driving license is issued today without any such counselling. This needs to be immediately changed – no new driving license should be given without the basic training in road etiquettes and taking a test of that through a stringent evaluation process. Strict law enforcement becomes vital at this point. Unfortunately, traffic police miserably fails in devising mechanism that prescribes and implements a cost to unruly behaviour on roads. Man by nature would calculate his risk and that being low would like to take a chance. Only a certainty that the risk is high by way of cost that he may try to avoid it.

Most developed cities in the world have this in-built 'cost to risky behaviour'. But we have reduced our democratic institutions into a sham. What do the traffic police do? They are enriching themselves at the cost of the public as speed money is the panacea for all traffic violations. It is common knowledge that crores of rupees are collected from traffic violators and it is a huge racket. So long as we have tolerance to such antisocial activities on the part of law-enforcement agencies, it will nearly be impossible to build a society that has respect for law and a concern for the fellow-beings.

I suggest that the Motor Vehicle Registration department should issue a sticker to every new owner to be affixed by him on the back screen of his car which would say, 'I love my dog but I don't bark like him'. But that would still not take care of scooterists and auto-rickshaw drivers. Then, what about all those trucks and tempos who carry, as if mandatorily, the slogan of 'Blow Horn'?

The civil society must take a call and build a movement to stop this nefarious practice afflicting our roads. In the long term, appropriate education in road etiquettes from early school days may help. As of now, regular campaigns in schools/colleges, communities and clubs are required to be undertaken. Crucial points will be creating mass awareness, educating and training motorists before issuing license, building inescapable cost into traffic violations and clipping the unbridled powers of traffic regulators by appointment of conscientious and willing citizens who would work as traffic magistrates and report violations on hotlines, which would be acted upon in a fast-track mode. The result would not be coming soon but not making a beginning is not an option any more.

Social Zombies

We have often wondered at the silence of others and sighed aloud, 'alas only if someone had spoken'! This silence has allowed injustice to be perpetrated and worst atrocities to have taken place without being resisted or even challenged. Many tragedies would have been averted if somebody at some point of time had tried to intervene. I am reminded of a very erudite Hindi poet, Dushyant who quite succinctly put the whole idea in two lines,

> *"ab kabhi is shahr me baraat ho ya vardaat*
> *Ab kisi bhi baat par khulti nahi hain khirkian"*
> (a marriage procession or an ugly incident in this town/
> just nothing invites opening of the windows anymore)

We hesitate in coming to the help of others, fail to raise our voice when we see injustice and vacillate in showing responsiveness as a citizen. The stories of accident victims lying unattended on the road, women being teased in the public transport, incidence of road rage or some unsocial behaviour taking place in full public view etc are common instances that are reported in the newspapers regularly. The passers-by just stop to satisfy their curiosity or to have a peek-a-boo for fun and carry on with their routine life. They carry the impression that whatever has happened will always occur to others and not to them. This typically reflects in apathetic response to social situations that cry for attention and thoughtful intervention.

Those who fail to come forward are oblivious to the looming peril. Their sense of social well-being is phony. There is little realization that they may face a similar danger one day when no one may come to their aid. The persons falling into this description can be called, for no better classification, as *'social zombies'*. They have cocooned themselves in a shell and become oblivious to the world outside. There is no attempt at internalizing the experiences and tribulations of the community they live with. It appears to be a case of disconnect between them and the social surroundings in which they live. Their perception is that the societal obligation is a drag and everyone has to fend for itself. They carry the consciousness of an illusionary autonomy that is not bound by any community obligation beyond the realm of family and friends. Thus there is no ownership of or accountability for the general good. Strangers are strangers and so be it.

We will not stop for one minute even if it is the matter of life and death for someone, what to talk of extending some small assistance to a neighbour in distress. This philosophy of life is nothing but nihilistic and will not lead us to the building of a happy society. The indifference to the plight of fellow citizens is amazing and defies explanation. In a manner of speaking the general apathy appears to be a function of social behaviour, inculcated not on community-mindedness but through self-seeking behaviour, exacerbated by selfish social mores. Should this not be a matter of concern; more so, should not there be an attempt to make a difference? Elie Wiesel had said, *"there may be times when we are powerless to prevent injustice. But there must never be a time when we fail to protest"*.And therefore, remonstrate we must if we want the society not to go to dogs.

Considering that our cities are neither part of a 'failed' nor that of a 'rogue State' or 'banana republic', the phenomenon is all the more embarrassing. We behave as if we will not live the other day and must make the most of it. Whether it is jumping the queue at every opportunity or elbowing our way to the reception, it is the same story all around. That cannot be the hallmark of a civil society. The symptoms recounted above typify the conduct of individuals in our cities today.

Pessimism is not good. Our society has many positive traits and exceptional resilience to bounce back when ever adversity grips the nation.

We can definitely make a difference. But we need to go in a campaign mode. Recognition of a problem is the first step in the direction of finding a solution. Let us become conscious that there is need for curative intervention to restore the 'social zombies' to health. Let a social resurgence become the driver for change; Information Education Campaign and Behaviour Change Communication its engine. Commitment to community or basic sense of responsibility to stand for community causes can be built up through education and practice. If 'small family norm' and 'literacy' can be promoted in this country through appropriate medium, volunteerism and communitarianism can be learnt as well. Family, schools, social clubs and community associations can be exhorted and relied upon to carry messages of this campaign. It is going to take not days or months but years.

The two previous programs, though quite successful were entirely government-driven till very recently and also devoid of, during its formative years, the support of the electronic and digital media. With the help of new technology the task can now be achieved better, faster and in lesser cost. Moreover, participation of the private sector and the civil society – now increasingly eager to support such causes – will without doubt take it through a fast-track mode and may show quicker results. There is need to emphasize building of character in the schools – the six pillars being trust-worthiness, respect, responsibility, fairness, caring and citizenship. Merely prescribing the course in schools will not do any good. There is need to have regular discussion on the theme of community-mindedness, civility and concern where young students are encouraged to participate, ask questions and give replies. Rewards and recognition should be considered for those coming up with innovative ideas and for conveying the substance of learning. There should be awards for teachers who excel in imparting such learning and in meeting their assigned tasks. Teachers themselves would first undergo orientation program before they are in a position to take the responsibility to train the young minds. Similarly communities will be encouraged to organize workshops where the subject will be debated and also best practices explained and showcased for the benefit of others. It is in these institutions that the seeds of volunteerism will be sown and will bear fruits for attaining our objective of revitalizing the 'social zombies'.

Thou Shalt Not Covet!

The infinite acquisition of material objects is one of the distinct characteristics of modern life. This is probably also linked to the overall economic progress that has brought about unprecedented prosperity for many more people who have extra money to splurge now than ever before. How far the Biblical tradition of shunning wealth is enforceable in the modern context is not clear. The Judeo-Christian tradition is not alone in advancing the philosophy of non-acquisition and its substitution by charity. Religious traditions of Hinduism, Sikhism, Islam, Buddhism, Jainism all harp eloquent on the virtues of austerity and promise returns ensuing from giving. All religions of the world endorse philanthropy in one form or the other.

Ethically speaking giving is considered an act of piety, a kindly and benevolent act. Intellectually it derives from the conviction that there is need to partly return to the society what is got from it. The trusts, endowments, foundations, grants etc. are set up by individuals and associations for purposes that are generally pious and charitable in nature. Religious endowments are also operated in our country by *Dharmartha* Trusts, *Wakf* Boards, *Samagams*, and Missionaries etc. who espouse similar causes. There are also non-religious organizations. Many of these are seen rushing with aid boxes to accident sites or to taking up relief during natural calamities.

The Indian tradition supports such activities as of considerable merit with assurances of return (*punya*) and benefits. Both the Bhakti and the Sufi traditions revolved around teachings that discouraged craving for worldly objects and emphasized devotion as means of salvation. But more importantly by speech and action, the proponents of these alternate philosophies exhorted their followers to shun worldly possessions and renounce materialism. Many Sufis did not believe in keeping anything for the next morning out of quantities received during the course of the day – the entire *nazrana*(offerings) was preferred to be disbursed by the same evening. Of course there was the more extreme instance of *sadhus*(ascetics) who literally renounced the world, wandered all around and abhorred keeping any material belongings.

Times have changed and now we hear of Corporate Social Responsibility (CSR), which is now generally integrated as business ethics by major companies, the idea being to show conscientiousness and responsibility and try to repay the society for its munificence. It is good to see some companies taking up social causes and organising events and programs to promote public health, education, or taking up direct interventions such as supporting poor children, women in distress etc. Even before such things came to be propagated and implemented widely by the likes of Bill & Melinda Gates Foundation and others, it had taken shape with big business houses and others who started the process of giving financial support to students in universities (Rhodes, Inlaks, McNamara, Commonwealth scholarships). Many international scholarships came to be given this way by big corporates in US and UK. With passage of time they became hugely popular and also prestigious as 'Seats' and 'Chairs' were established in reputed universities the world over. AMU and BHU, the two Central Indian Universities were mostly run on charities and endowments in their formative years. Talking of Industry, TATAs were known for their ethical practices and contributions to charity. Azim Premji Foundation is one of the pioneers of most organized work in this sector in India in recent years.

It is said that comparisons are odious but they could still be attempted not to criticize but to learn. As per an estimate, the size of charity in USA has touched $ 300 billion. Now that is stupendous compared to anything we have. Our trillion dollar economy, with all the concerns about the lack of redistributive justice, and constant focus of flak due to the stashing away of huge unaccounted offshore wealth, can nowhere be equated with such gigantic scale. The trend for organized charity in India is still quite nascent. Giving has not caught on and is still far from fashionable. Talking of CSR, the distinction between genuine efforts – both by way of quantum provided and the level of commitment – and the need for publicity is sometimes blurred. Some with their thirst for publicity would be happy by paying lip service and by taking up only such projects as would ensure a wide media coverage.

The explanation can be found when we look at institutions of religious denominations/individuals, especially when they are compared with the West. It is different both in quality and quantity and that is what calls for introspection. It is less inclusive here and dictated by more restrictive considerations, namely for instance to help the poor from their own community. The amount kept apart is also small compared to the size of the problem or the number seeking help. Since the genesis and derive to give charity comes from religious conviction, the choice gets limited and naturally falls on "your own folks". The lack of social commitment is discernible here. Our religiosity and caste consciousness is the biggest barrier to inclusive progression in this sector like in other areas as well. It militates against an all-embracing commitment to genuine social causes. Since volunteerism becomes victim to an exclusivist outlook, the response to social deficits becomes inadequate. The trek to post-modern reflection on societal needs calls for a more eclectic and catholic approach towards charity. Since charity begins at home, each one of our broad-based contribution to the cause shall have value and the first step in that direction could be the harbinger of the most profound future changes.

Time to Revive
Fundamental Duties

The American business magnet and philanthropist, John Rockefeller noted, *"Every right implies a responsibility; every opportunity, an obligation; every possession, a duty"*. In the renewed emphasis and weightage being given to governance in the country, the duties of citizens become as important as the role of Government and its agencies. The citizenry must therefore imbibe in full measure awareness and consciousness of its role and responsibility.

We may recall that a set of Fundamental Duties was inserted as Article 51 A in Part IV A of the Constitution of India by the 42nd amendment in 1976. There were various other amendments, some of which were struck down or repealed subsequently, however, not the Fundamental Duties. These have not caused any misgivings or reservations in the minds of the people, or the Apex Court that later came to adjudicate over many of the 42nd amendments. Though never challenged, regrettably, these duties have been totally ignored in the scheme of things of our country, perhaps because the 42nd amendment itself got discredited due to the excesses of the emergency era.

So much negativity surrounded the Emergency and the massive constitutional amendments carried out during that period that the best also got blurred and we could not separate the wheat from the chaff. No Government in the succeeding three decades tried to promote the fundamental duties, what to talk of even mentioning them in any routine discourse. Thus this wonderful product of the 'dark days' totally disappeared from the socio-political narrative of the country and was not found attractive enough despite the maxim that lotus blooms in the mud.

Far removed in time and space, we should now be able to take a more detached perspective. Much water has flown down the Yamuna and all other rivers of the country since those 'dark days'. We may therefore take a fresh view of the fundamental duties of citizens and relate it to the context of improved governance. Some of these may appear idealistic but worth emulating nonetheless. Lest we forget, 67 years is not a long time in the history of a nation and we are still evolving as a democratic modern nation. Positioning the nation's psyche on a healthy intellectual base of personal responsibility of every citizen should be considered a constructive intervention.

Let us examine some of the fundamental duties: "to abide by the constitution and respect its ideals and institutions; to uphold and protect the sovereignty, unity and integrity of India; to defend the country and render national service when called upon to do so; to promote harmony and the spirit of common brotherhood amongst all the people of India transcending religious, linguistic and regional diversities; to renounce practices derogatory to the dignity of women; to value and preserve the rich heritage of our composite culture; to protect and improve the natural environment including forests, lakes, and wild-life and to have compassion for living creatures; to safeguard property and abjure violence; ......".

Aren't they quite unexceptional and contemporaneous in intent and purpose? Intellectual honesty demands that we agree to their relevance even after thirty years. Talk of government services, maintenance of public infrastructures, civic standards, traffic rules, adherence to law etc. and we can't but think of the lack of a sense of responsibility on the part of the citizens. Seen in this context, we may find that the general apathy, indifference, negligent behaviour and thoughtless acts contribute to the unmaking of governance initiatives. Many of the ills in the society today including physical and verbal attacks on others stem from the fact that there is no consensus to follow a self-imposed code of conduct.

The fundamental duties basically prescribe a Code of Conduct for the citizens and try to endorse and encourage a proactive social stance. The nation and the society provide care and sustenance to the citizens to lead a good life and to grow. This contribution largely remains one sided because there is no return from the citizens to the society. We are happy in taking but reluctant in giving back.

This inadequacy relates to attitudes which develop over a period of time. It is a question to ponder how some nationalities make remarkable progress while some are left behind. The western civilisation subjugated and conquered the East during the 17th and 18th centuries by dint of their superior political and cultural organisations. Their military might and better technology were the products of their reformed political and cultural institutions – post Renaissance, Reformation, and Industrial Revolution. Their ideas of exploration and navigation also came from better institutions, which helped them in conquering the world.

Since history repeats itself, with wisdom and learning, we may take a cue and learn to fix our institutions. The progression of institutions is a continuum and depends as much on the Government of the day as on the citizenry. The process may start with internal rejuvenation that promotes and honours certain duties on the part of each citizen of the country. The transformation would happen in a generation's time through intensive education, training and practice of civic duties. Mahatma Gandhi said, *"It is wrong and immoral to seek to escape the consequences of one's acts"*. Let's try to build soft skills – for creating an enlightened citizenry – and gain competitive advantage in this fast moving world.

ESSENTIALLY CIVIL

North Block, New Delhi- The Seat of Power

Civil Services through the Ages

The role of civil service has undergone tremendous change from the time of the British from whom we inherited the institution to the present age. It has been evolving all along and is today largely seen as facilitator rather than ruler and dispenser of justice as in the earlier era. At the dawn of independence it was retained for the governance of the country by national leaders like Nehru and Patel, owing to the reputation of the civil service being fair, firm, steadfast, honest and efficient. It was the question of perspective then and is still a mute question as to how much of that confidence was well-placed.

In the earliest era, recruits to the hallowed Indian Civil Service (ICS) were only English. Later the service was thrown open to the Indians as well. With passage of time, the ICS came to be conferred with tremendous admiration and respect – the young dashing horse borne lads were the lure of all, the most eligible bachelors in India in whose hands the maharajas and *nawabs* would vie with each other to give hands of their daughters. Incidentally, the trend has remained to this day except that the craze for 'adoption' is now to be found amongst the successors of maharajas and *nawabs* – we all know who we are talking about. After their initial stints in the districts as representatives of the Imperial State in all its glorified ramifications – administering, ruling, dispensing justice, policing etc., they were summoned to state capital to assist the governor or to the national capital for aiding the Viceroy, as the case may be.

The concept of ruling, very rightly has since disappeared, even as the ICS morphed into the Indian Administrative Service (IAS). The aura and respect for the new *avtar* continued for some years but started gradually to dissipate in the succeeding decades owing to various factors. In the meanwhile there was paradigm shift in what the civil servants were doing in the discharge of their responsibilities. The administrative machinery of the welfare state had been expanding manifold – role of the civil service was now more for program implementation and execution in the field and assisting the political executive in policy formulations. The democratization of polity has meant not only diversification of job responsibilities but also considerable 'dilution of authority' in the sense it was known earlier. Now the 'power', if at all, is to be shared or at best enjoyed with the blessing of the masters.

While it may be true as regards fading of authority, the diversification of job of the members of the Civil Service at the higher levels has meant being entrusted with duties which are ranging from banking to civil aviation, mining, defence procurement, food security to organizing games; in fact anything or everything which the Government may be required to handle. To that extent the experience gained by Civil Servants is awesome and they are comparable to the best from Private Sectors like the CEOs and CMDs of top Multinational Companies.

Even at the middle and lower ranks, the responsibility is now more towards development initiatives including social, educational, health and social welfare measures of the Government. This gives an opportunity to the officers to contribute to the development of the State/or District in which they are serving. There are large numbers of dedicated, committed, hardworking and sincere Civil Servants whose contribution to governance must be acknowledged. At the same time there is no dearth of moles who bring bad name to the Civil Service. These are persons obsessed with fascination for money and power and therefore adopt dubious means for perpetuating their self-interest. It is the former category that we celebrate and applaud with the hope that their tribe thrive while those in the second category get marginalized, so that the reputation of Civil Servants is maintained and prospers.

State of the Nation –
Newer Context

The developed democracies of the world debate subjects like efficiency versus accountability - a discretionary framework. Our problem is different and we are perhaps far away from getting into a debate like this because unfortunately, in people's perception, the Indian bureaucracy is neither efficient nor really accountable. We may perhaps better talk of efficiency and outcome as important elements of governance; rather also, the process through which that objective is sought to be realized. Efficiency is easily recognizable and has a high value put on it by all — but the market is its greatest votary. Being both the driver and the beneficiary of an efficient system, market would prefer and always extend support for efficiency, even if, at some additional cost.

No wonder then that an efficient officer is more respected than an honest officer. A deviant behaviour in terms of personal integrity would attract less attention if credentials of an officer as a capable and competent go-getter are settled. Since public services have to, and should, meet certain standards and time-frame, it is natural, practical and perhaps justifiable as well that the trade-off between efficiency and integrity increasingly becomes acceptable to many and even to the system itself. If an honest officer happens to be efficient, that is a silver lining. But if he is honest and inefficient, he becomes a liability to the system as such. He is spoken of in disparaging terms by colleagues and juniors; perhaps such a person is generally unpopular as much within his peer group and organization as in his own extended family. We may say something like, *"na khuda hi milaa, na wisaal-e-sanam"* (neither he attained union with the god, nor with his beloved). Cynical words though, what does the poor thing do with a reputation like that?

The issue has now reached center-stage as reflected in the sudden turn of electoral politics experienced in one of the states, clearly fought on the plank of corruption and governance – in fact, that was the USP of one of the political groupings that caught the imagination of the people like never before and this new development paid dividend too. We do not know if this change will become harbinger of a new hope for rejuvenation of society and politics, much sought after by right-thinking persons in and outside the bureaucracy. However, the development is important in the context of people's longing for and involvement in the affairs of the state and society.

The public has relied too long on the bounty of the State, without making exertions for correcting the ills. Dr. AllamaIqbal, the composer of our national song recorded this lamentably, *"Khuda ne aaj tak us qaum ki haalat nahi badli//na ho jisko khyaal aap apni haalat ke badalne ka"*! (God never transforms a community//who itself is not concerned with improving its lot). Nani Palkiwala once said, *"Eternal vigilance is the price of liberty"*! But we hardly maintain any vigilance. The change we so desperately seek in our public life, the way we do things and the improvement in our general ethical standards, would happen only if we be the change that we want, as was observed by the father of the nation. The privilege based dispensation must give way to merit-based recognition. Swami Vivekananda was miffed by what he called the 'son-in-law' mentality. Duties of citizens as enshrined in our constitution have remained embedded in those pages. In a moment like this, they may also be dusted and brought out of the cupboard and put in practice. Besides, the new force of public eagerness and enthusiasm must be relied upon by the bureaucracy to strengthen honest delivery of public services. Bureaucratic professionalism demands that this opportunity must not be allowed to dissipate and disintegrate for lack of timely recognition by the Institution that is willed and mandated to be in the vanguard of that task.

Reinventing Oneself

Perhaps it was Carlyle who said, *"Give me a man who sings at his work"*. Talking especially of the government offices, fatigue or more simply lack of interest in the assigned work or office environment is common. This happens perhaps because we do not question ourselves or introspect. The government officials should truly experience a humbler existence owing to this opportunity ordained to them that empowers them to be useful to others. Generally contrary is the case – whereby they start enjoying power over others. The question to ask is whether that is the purpose of life – power and money? Obtaining two morsels cannot be the objective of our life; it has a bigger meaning. Living this way would provide livelihood somehow but that would be devoid of substance and meaning. How to see the bigger picture? What is it that is to be sought and reclaimed from countless competing elements clamoring for our attention?

The point that is being made here is that one has to take a call about one's purpose of life and that determines one's attitude to work and what would be the quality of output as also the shape of deliverables. Besides, there is constantly the issue of right and wrong and occasionally a conflict even between two rights; also how far should an employee go in the discharge of his official duties. The real difficulty is, face to face with a dilemma, not knowing the way to proceed! It is not easy to find answers to these issues without serious self-reflection. But the exertion to reach that level is worthy of consideration.

Not only idealistically, but also practically it is required, to obviate the law of diminishing returns from applying to governance issues.

There are conditions that can only be attained by a supra-consciousness and by rising to a level of inspiration that can help in finding the real meaning of life. The framework provided by David Osborne & Ted Gaebler in 'Reinventing Government' prescribes that the reinvention process is most likely to be achieved by five strategies, cogently categorized as Core, Consequence, Customer, Control and Culture strategies (five 'Cs'). Putting them together and relying upon them gives a deep understanding of what works and what does not. We are thus talking of developing a different work culture.

Eckhart Tolle, commenting about his own book, 'A New Earth: Awakening to Your Life's Purpose', makes a very significant statement, "... *it can only awaken those who are ready*". Thus it is entirely up to us as to how much we take from our experiences. The idea is to undertake a journey of the 'self' through the mesh of myriad desires, fears and predilections, and yet be able to discover a life that gives a meaning; a sense that involves self-actualization for aiming at and attaining higher goals. That alone could be the real take-away lesson in a journey towards internalization of one's life and experiences. A higher level of consciousness is therefore desirable as well as attainable. We need to develop a vision to strive for excellence, not in a narrow, selfish sense but in a broader sense, to be able to give to others the best possible or at least what we expect to get from others.

Men and women would not succeed unless a vision is created, a vision with inner strength and endowed with purpose and meaning that would enable them in steering the processes. Supervision in government departments should be such that it does not create bottlenecks in the workflow. Something forced upon by others or by circumstances does not give the same result. The employees who do not work at optimum levels are those who have the work thrust upon them. Creating ownership is, therefore of paramount importance. Once they take psychological ownership in the work situation, thereby manifesting entrepreneurial traits, effects will transform – an entrepreneur is one who uses his resources to maximize efficiency and effectiveness. The need is to discover the fiber within and strengthen it, so as to seek fulfillment through psychological ownership of the Organization. Discovering this fiber has to be a key deliverable in any training programs for officers.

The focus should be to put the citizen at the center. Mahatma Gandhi's talisman must be considered the best prescription for attaining this objective. Rules, institutions, offices are for addressing the needs of the people. Once divested of that centricity they lose their meaning. Hence the endeavor should be to draw the officials near this approach. The mindset needs to undergo an alteration. Luckily there is a change filtering into the system through the mechanisms of e-governance and legal requirement of the Right to Information Act. Our role would be to strengthen this move towards transparency and accountability along with result-oriented outcomes by encouraging thinking and self-reflection.

Civil Service & Leadership Role

An attempt is made here to envision leadership role of the civil service through the prism of some expert elucidations and experiential comments. Dr. AllamaIqbal, the great Indian poet-philosopher eulogized a leader in these words, *"Nigah buland, sukhan dilnawaz, jaan pursoz//yehi hain rakht-e-safar meer-e-karvaan ke liye"*!(A lofty vision, an endearing expression, a warm heart//these are the gears of expedition for the leader of a caravan). Civil Service is nothing but administrative leadership. A team excels or fails depending on the qualities or the lack of it in leadership. The leadership of civil administration is indeed as important in times of peace as it is for the military commanders in times of war. Whether it is urgent fire-fighting or an important matter or even a routine calling, what comes from above contains a significant downward message, for the followers, sometimes neutral, occasionally right or even wrong. That is the defining appellation of leadership.

The efficacy of leadership counts from the smallest unit of administration – managed by the incumbent at Taluka/SDM level at the beginning of the career, to the top – Secretary level, over the next 30-35 years. Therefore, seeds that get embedded during the formatting years in the psyche of the members of the civil service are most likely to survive and play a crucial role over next three-four decades. If these were healthy earlier, the future flowers and fruits are most likely to be well-grown too.

A leader by very definition has to be optimistic. He/she cannot be or should not resemble a character from a Greek or Shakespearean tragedy or a replica of Shere Khan or Lord Voldemort. Leader must have a pleasing disposition, positive countenance and know how to smile sincerely. Phyllis Diller, the well-known American stage artist and stand-up comedian famously remarked, *"A smile is a curve that sets everything straight."* Charles Gordy, a Harvard Law School teacher could not be far from truth when he said, *"A smile is an inexpensive way to improve your looks."* Our administrative leadership needs some schooling in the business of smiling.

The second important attribute of a leader has to be positivity in attitude. Catherine Ponder, inspirational writer has this to say for developing a positive personality, *"What you radiate outward in your thoughts, feelings, mental pictures and words, you attract into your life"*. A positive leader leads his team from the front and is able to navigate his charge with much ease through willing cooperation of his team. It helps him in taking an impersonal and detached view of issues and persons and therefore reaching better decisions.

A leader must maintain ethical standards in his supervisory role, and while allocating works to his juniors. Kim Cameron, an expert on organizational virtuousness as quoted in a recent newspaper column explained that the work is related to meaningfulness when it (a) has an impact on the well-being of humans (b) is associated with an important virtue or personal value (c) has an impact that extends beyond the time-frame or creates a ripple effect, and (d) builds supportive relationship or a sense of community in people.

A good leader is neither self-centric nor unreasonably demanding. Schon L. Beechler, a noted teacher on the subject of organizational behaviour lamented, *"Some executives become so entangled by the enormity of their position that they lose sight of their role in helping their employees sustain their energy and commitment to what is meaningful in their lives."* Leader should find ways to connect or reconnect their employees to what is important – to a purpose, to a universal search for meaning – and building their confidence for coming to work every day.

It may be added that dignity of self and that of those working for the leader should be his/her immediate concern. Viktor Frankl, a neurologist and a psychiatrist, a holocaust survivor, in his book, 'Man's Search for Meaning', despite undergoing intense horror and pain prayed, even in the face of imminent death, to *"hold on to my dignity when everything else was getting lost"*. This dignity cannot be denied to the subordinates by a good leader, and is possible only when he conducts himself with the same poise.

Reflections in the Line of Duty

A career in the Government is not really as enviable as many might think. It is not even a 'crown of thorns', in that, there you at least have a crown; here it is more often brickbats, notwithstanding the much-touted so-called job security. It is said that the government is a machine wherein employees are like small cogs. Looking back, one does not always exactly get the feeling of merely being a cog. There are moments of elation as well, especially when one's contribution is appreciated for having been able to fulfill certain responsibility to a cause, a group or an individual in need. To quote, Henry Longfellow *"we judge ourselves by what we feel capable of doing, while others judge us by what we have already done"*.

Thus more important is not what we think of ourselves but what others perceive us to be. Generally we tend to take a self-righteous position whereby our acts or deeds appear to be all done either 'with good intentions' or 'in good faith'. Also probably we carry the burden of vanity, may be unconsciously; sometimes having the illusion of performing a divinely ordained task. Subjective though it may sound, a bright and smart bureaucrat would be able to find enough rationale to establish this fame for himself and the justification for such a position. We routinely come across several high-flying officers who have led the world to seriously believe about their indispensability to the system under their nose. They are successful in creating a halo around their persona through hero-worships. Perhaps, this is also because we like to hear such words of adulations.

Exposed to such sycophancies and with passage of time we start believing what we initially wanted to hear from others. Many of us may have played important roles in governance in the past and looked at it with some pride but in all fairness these should have been looked at as part of our overall job responsibility. But that not being so any good work done by an officer is taken by the people to be an extra-ordinary contribution of that officer and hence the accolades. It does give moments of elation to a person so acclaimed. Though, sometimes praises are also showered where they do not belong.

The reverse is often true as well, i.e. a great contribution of some extra-ordinary works not getting recognized, either by oversight, or because the officer concerned is not the one who blows his own trumpet, let alone being media/network savvy. Either way, we get to find people who are affected or hurt by the impact of this rush for name and fame generally and money in some cases as well. There must be ways to address or come to terms with such situations.

We may try to have the consciousness to reevaluate one's role in terms of the meaning of life. The point is whether to react ardently or face the calling rationally. Rationalism is not the medium for all our dreams. Actions guided only by rationality may lead to mechanical reactions. We know that man does not live for bread alone. There are situations and needs that can only be attained by supra-consciousness and by rising to a level of inspiration that can help in finding the real meaning of life. So we ask whether the purpose of life is only to earn money. Does life not have some bigger meaning? Should we not try to see the larger picture? The idea is to be 'awakened and ready', so as to undertake a journey of the self' through the mesh of myriad fears and predilections, and yet be able to discover a life that gives a meaning that is not abstract but involves self-actualization for aiming at and attaining higher goals.

We need to develop a vision to strive for excellence, not in a narrow, selfish sense but in a broader sense, to be able to give to others the best possible or at least what we expect to get from them. A higher level of consciousness is attainable. Eckhart Tolle tells us that this consciousness can be achieved through what he calls *'awakened doing'* – these being 'acceptance', 'enjoyment' and 'enthusiasm'. This is not a utopian concept. We know it from experience that the work we do best is the one we like most. Something that is kind of forced upon us by others or by circumstances does not give the same result. Once we take psychological ownership in the work situation, thereby manifesting entrepreneurial traits, effects will transform. The need is to discover the fiber within and strengthen it, so as to seek fulfillment through psychological ownership of the Organization.

Civil Service – Reputation, Efficacy and Challenges

Shri Gopal Krishna Gandhi, ex-bureaucrat and ex-Governor, an impeccable iconic personality and an erudite scholar, had quoted in his column on the eve of Independence Day last August, *"Everywhere money is King not the voter, not the Constitution but money; when something or someone is King what becomes of the Republic"* – the statement was purported to have been voiced with angst by Pundit Nehru. The context of course was large scale use of money and muscle power in elections those days; that happened despite the control and management of elections vesting largely with the civil service, or because of it – a clear failure of constitutional duty. Luckily, electoral reforms and improvement in election processes have altered the situation to a great extent. The fair and free election is being delivered today by the same government machinery. It is in this background that we may cite from the horse's mouth.

Shri P.K. Misra, the then Establishment Officer, GOI and later Secretary, DOPT exhorted public servants to inculcate certain values: Patriotism and upholding National Pride, Allegiance to the Constitution and Law of the nation, Objectivity, Impartiality, Honesty, Diligence, Courtesy, Transparency and Integrity. Shri Sanjeev Sabhlok who quit the IAS some years ago lamented, "the system is incorrigible and cannot be corrected. It needs to be rebuilt from scratch on first-principle reform." Some while critiquing the civil service from within have taken satirical routes like M.K. Kaw in 'Bureaucrazy' and Upamanyu Chatterjee in 'The Mammaries of the Welfare State'. Both have been non-sparing to their own ilk but the latter has been more scathing.

If good comes to adorn civil service responsibility for bad will also have to be taken. The point to seriously consider is why governance in India is derided so much. Why the 'Steel Frame' is under constant attack for being sloth, unresponsive and corrupt? The class is often referred derogatorily as parasitical, conceited, self-righteous, corrupt and even incompetent. On the other hand, many in the bureaucracy feel that they are more sinned against than sinning.

It was clear from the post-freedom era itself that inclusive economic growth was one of the national objectives and various programs were launched by the Government to address this. If that did not happen and the public delivery could not improve through measurable outcomes after more than half a century, and the country remained beset with wide regional and economic disparities, the blame has to be shared by the policy makers, planners and executors, bulk of which comprises the decision-making and cutting-edge level officialdom. Institution building, capacity enhancement and honest diligent work could have helped in reducing poverty, enlarging primary education, pushing better health cover for the masses and thereby galvanizing the human resource as engines of growth. This failure and shoddy policy implementation decades after decades are difficult to explain. To top it, one has lost count of alleged scams in the country. It is not surprising that we are ranked at the bottom of the list by Transparency International, so also on the scales of Ease of doing Business and HDI. Today the public perception is extremely negative about the personal integrity of Civil Servants at large.

The above scenario gives a gloomy picture and can be a dampener for any upright, enthusiastic young officer looking for a bright career in the Civil Service. But there is no reason to despair. To restore optimism and to generate hope and confidence among the people, civil service may need to reinvent itself. And one of the ways for this could be to re-imagine the 'Idea of India'.

For that, we may go back to the presentation of Shri P.K. Misra, i.e. truly respect the Constitution of India and build up the national pride - may show the way to rejuvenate the civil service. Let this concept be relied upon through focus on the idea of India to constitutional and moral commitment of the State for the well-being of all its citizens. All the training in financial analysis and project management techniques, international pedagogy and exposure to world-wide best practices will not be able to make a dent without first developing a humane face and deep commitment of the bureaucracy to be the change-agents. There cannot be a magic wand to leapfrog the development processes. But the beginning may be made by building ethical standards in bureaucracy. The processes have to be reengineered to conform to transparency, impartiality, efficiency and accountability. In the long run, the foundation has to come from an ethical framework laid in the class rooms of young boys and girls, for achieving national goals through a generation of righteous citizens of this great country.

Building up an Ethical Framework for Government Sector

The country is at a crucial juncture of economic growth, with aspirations and forecast to be the third largest economy of the world in times to come. That prospect is not too off the mark as we have been doing better than many other countries during the last couple of years. However, it is not only the GDP that is important for a country's all round development but also the increase in per capita income, thereby ensuring a more equitable distribution of the gains of economic progress. It was believed that with liberalization and globalization of the economy and as the national income will rise, all sections of the society will gain and would be able to get a share in the rising wealth of the country, i.e. through a trickledown effect. So more sections of the society would be benefited and would be part of an inclusive growth through a redistributive process. After twenty years, that hope, as is apparently clear now, has not been realised. The number of poor living in squalor and sub-human conditions has actually risen while certain sections of the society have become richer and richer. It is in this background that increasingly we talk of transparency and accountable administration for good governance.

There have been frequent talks of governance-deficit in this country. Perhaps the real reason for this is deficit in the ethical standards of all concerned, public or private that affects governance at all levels and worst sufferers, in any such scenario, are always the poor. We may try to analyse what is wrong there and how it adversely impacts the distribution of economic gains. Many years ago, a late Prime Minister had lamented that only 15% of the grant reaches the poor. That assumption is considered correct in the public perception even today. That is the tragedy of our liberal democracy. Despite several healthy democratic institutions, we have not been able to reverse this tide; if anything it has continued to spread all across. Not surprisingly, while we count quite low down on World Human Development Index; our ranking as per the Transparency International, in terms of corruption in public life, is equally dismal. Corruption and inefficiency are roundly responsible for the current state of our public services and skewed distributive processes.

Since the execution and implementation of public policies and delivery of government schemes are the preserve of government officials, the responsibility for slowness, inefficiency, pilferage, non-performance and quality aspects have to be borne by them alone. The inadequacy there happens because of the lack of adherence to ethical standards by public servants in their belief and practices. Since the salary structure in the government has also improved compared to the earlier times, the lame excuse of not being able to meet the two ends, as if that facetious pretext can justify inefficiency and corruption, does not buy. In fact many of these employees have their spouses also working; the average household income of the government employees is actually not too bad. If they still find it difficult to live within their rightful means and seek extra gratification, then clearly the problem lies elsewhere. Gandhiji had observed that there is enough on Earth for everybody's need but not enough for everybody's greed. Unless and until greed is controlled, there cannot be a long term solution of our ills and that control could only come through absorption and adoption of ethical standards in the national life along with vigorous institutional enforcement on government officials first, and on the private sector thereafter. But then who will bell the cat?

Government Employees and Organizational Citizenship Behaviour

It struck me recently that my office car driver was rarely resorting to honking, over speeding or jumping the red light etc. while driving to office(s). I have also observed him noticing with the corner of his eyes – with some degree of trepidation as also jealous admiration the audacity of other motorists and his own incapacity to be able to do that – some motorists speeding off while this poor chap obediently waits at the traffic junctions. Perhaps he knew how much I hated these mindless habits of motorists. But permit to say that often government car drivers are found to be less inclined to unnecessary honking; they are also more disciplined and particular in following traffic rules. This has given some food for thought. One may assume that there is a basic structure of responsibility inherent in most government employees – not for any altruist but for reasons of obligatory nature of duty – which as the base line could be further developed to promote certain sets of responsible social behaviour in them, for others to follow. To begin with this minor responsible trait may be used to build up greater participation of these men and women for promoting social causes.

Let us for the moment, not talk of the rent-seeking behaviour that the government servants are often accused of. After all, has it not been said that people are not just black and white but have shades of grey as well. It is the grey shade that is being emphasized here. We may bank on Organizational Citizenship Behaviour for attaining some of the objectives.

We may have a brief look at the conceptual framework developed by some theorists. Organizational Citizenship Behaviour (OCB) may be relied upon to explain employees' attitude to volunteerism and social participation.Dennis W. Organ defined OCB as individual behavior that is discretionary, not directly or explicitly recognized by the formal reward system and that in the aggregate promotes the effective functioning of the organization. The core of OCB was identified by him as altruism, courtesy, sportsmanship, conscientiousness and civic virtue.The concept suggests that OCB is not an enforceable requirement of the role or the job description of the employee; rather a matter of personal choice and its omission does not entail any punishment. Thus it may be said to extend to a government organization that is trying to achieve certain social objectives. There are two dimensions of this; intra-organizational volunteerism, in support of social security initiatives that are planned and implemented by the government, and inter-organizational volunteerism, characterized by voluntary activities of individual employees for the common good.It is a discretionary individual behavior, one that is not enforceable requirement of the job or not included in the formal reward system. Such behavior is a matter of personal choice and its omission is not considered punishable. These may be cultivated through motivational programs.It may be suggested that it can increase the value and therefore, the competitive advantage of the government programs by increasing the alignment between the social cause and implementation strategy.

Talking about his vision of India NaniPalkhivala observed, *"While eternal vigilance is undoubtedly the price of liberty, yet in a more profound sense eternal responsibility is also part of the price of liberty"*. We may recall that the sense of responsibility was sought to be ingrained by incorporating Fundamental Duties in the constitution; unfortunately though it has been totally ignored since then due to Emergency excesses. Is it not possible to put the government servants at the vanguard of such a social resurgence? Not to miss the point, renewing emphasis on OCB and fundamental duties may be a good point to begin the rejuvenation. An attempt may be made to make a beginning with the cognitive awareness of this class, which is not small in number and otherwise also bound by certain codes of conduct. We may close the subject by reiterating the objective of first putting the government employees to such a course correction.

THE IDEA OF INDIA

In the Memory of the Unsung Heroes

The world colonialism had started declining by the middle of the 20th century and especially in the wake of Second World War and its aftermath. However, freedom to the suppressed nationalities came at a huge cost. In fact enormous sacrifices went behind such struggles for freedom. Large number of faceless people laid down their lives fighting the imperialists or the occupation forces in many countries. These martyrs are remembered by their co-nationalists with deep sense of gratitude and affection. They are sought to be immortalised by erecting beautiful memorials in their honour by the grateful citizens all over the world. Vast multitudes gather at such sites and interact with each other, sharing poignant thoughts and memories.

We, in India, have scant respect for the 'unknown soldier'. The exception we have made are for the national leaders like Mahatma Gandhi (Rajghat) and Pundit Nehru (Shantivan), and some others – they are sprawling and serene but devoid of grandeur. They are not made to facilitate interaction among large number of people in public place. They neither evoke national pride or nationalistic sentiments. These memorials have acquired more of a sanctimonious or rather ritualistic character. They are quintessentially neither icons of national identification nor epitomes of cultural fervour. It can be said that the memorial for the unknown soldiers is non-existent in our country.

It is terribly sad that we have forgotten these fallen heroes who sacrificed everything in blind love of their motherland.

Who are these unknown soldiers? Though hopelessly belated, let us remember them now when we are celebrating the 150 years of the first freedom movement in this country. They are to be found in the statistics or records (archives) of the so-called law enforcement agencies of the Establishment. They were the real patriots who suffered deprivation, torture, misery, indignities and death in their own country at the hand of foreign occupiers. They would not have the slightest hope of any reward as there was no expectation of immediate freedom in their minds then; rather imminent death was a more likely outcome of such struggles. But they were fuelled by a fire to free their motherland from the shackles of slavery. There were amongst them also those who wanted to avenge the attack on the dignity of their motherland. Even those laid down their lives who were votaries of non-violence and who did not hurl a single stone at the British forces. It is easy to say 10 dead or 200 wounded. Its real import unfolds when this is understood in terms of an individual or family's trauma and calamity whose bread-winner is killed.

But most of these fighting for recovering the lost destiny and wounded pride of their motherland were anonymous soldiers. They were not well-known persons and hence cannot be identified. Most of them or their kin, for the same reason, did not receive even freedom fighters' pension. They did not care for the safety and wellbeing of their families – unlike the present breed of politicians who within their life time make provision for the next four generations.

Who are we talking about? We are looking at all those who laid down their lives on the streets during the freedom struggle any time from 1905 to 1947 and much before this - we must not forget the first war of Indian Independence in 1857, and many other occasions later on like the martyrdom at the Jallianwala Bagh and those who died during the peak of Quit India Movement in 1942. How can we forget all those who went to the gallows at a very young age? They gave their 'today' (life) for India's 'tomorrow'. But for their sacrifices we would have perhaps waited for many more years to gain freedom. How many beautiful and imposing structures or public spaces have we created in their sacred memories that will give us pride? The medieval monarchs built mausoleums in the memory of their near and dear ones and later British constructed memorials for their fallen soldiers. But we have failed in honouring our real heroes who died on the streets or in British prisons.

Do we have no sense of gratitude for these hundreds of thousands of selfless, faceless, and nameless persons, who did not chose the softer option of collaborating with the British and did not allow themselves to be restrained by filial affection and responsibilities? Let us ask ourselves what we have done for the perpetuation of their memories or at least to make the young generation aware of the immense sacrifices of these people. Do they not merit being part of the national consciousness? Is lack of this awareness and shared nationalistic consciousness the reason for many of the societal ills, e.g. corruption, lack of commitment to the cause of nation building?

It was poet Revolutionary Ram Prasad Bismil who composed, *"shaheedon ki chitaon per lagenge har baras mele/ watan per marne walon ka yehi baqi nishan hoga"*! (the graves of martyrs will be places of annual congregation/this will be the markers of those who laid their lives for the nation). Unfortunately this is not happening; perhaps also, because there are none (martyr's landmarks). *'Melas'*(festivals) are organised, we must admit without undermining their contribution, only at the *'samadhis'*(graves) of national leaders whose third or fourth generations today have power, good time and money, whereas the successive generations of those freedom fighters who died on the streets, on the scaffold or in British jails have been overlooked and are mostly anonymous. It is sad that we have forgotten our martyrs.

No imposing structures have been made to commemorate their memories and to keep the young generation informed of what these selfless, unsung soldiers did for this country. No attempt has been made to instil or knit national consciousness of the younger generations around the memory of these icons and architects of our freedom struggle – this would have been meaningful in the context of our losing endeavour to provide role-models to the youngsters. If we hold our head high today, it is because of the sacrifices of these martyrs. We must remember the oft-quoted maxim, 'those who forget history are condemned to live by it'. We may open a new leaf in nation building by reviving the indomitable spirit of the martyrs by preserving and perpetuating their memory and thereby safeguard and strengthen our Republic.

The Red Fort, Delhi - Crying for a Martyr's Memorial

Reminiscing Along with the Heroes of Freedom Struggle

Watching the Republic Day march-past on the Raj path has always been a matter of pride and joy. The recently observed 66th anniversary of the Republic rekindled the blissful memories connected to the celebrations of the Golden Jubilee of Indian Independence in 1997. I was then posted in Andaman Administration. An opportunity dawned to interact with venerated freedom fighters. The Administration was observing the occasion in a big way and invited freedom fighters to be part of the celebration from the 'mainland'; that is how the rest of the physical landmass of the country is known in the islands.

The term, 'mainland', I found sweet and amazing at the same time, when compared with different appellation (like India) given to it in some other territories that are physically not so apart. Coming back to our subject, the freedom fighters were brought by special flight to Port Blair escorted for reasons of their advance age by a companion each, most of them being in their 70s and 80s. It was inspiring to hear these heroes of yesteryears recalling their exploits who despite their frail frames exhumed rare strength, pride, enthusiasm and warmth. Many of them had spent their youthful years in the dreaded Cellular jail on the island with much sufferings and untold miseries. Port Blair for them now was a pious place that had all the glory of a

61

tirathsthan(pilgrim place). Being a witness and a participant in that carnival was a matter of pride and privilege for those of us who were then serving in Andaman.

We tried not to miss any opportunity to hear stories of those days. The drudgery of captivity in such a far-flung territory, cruelty of prison officials, made poignant by coarse food, murky water, lack of medical care and inhospitable climate was further aggravated by the malevolent presence of dangerous pests and reptiles of all hue; mortality was very high. Many also suffered heightened brutalities during the Japanese occupation of the islands from 1942 to 1945.

We heard of a horrifying story related to a surviving islander actually living off a human corpse on an abandoned island for few days during the Japanese occupation of Andaman Islands. Unhealthy labour prisoners were taken in boats, shot and dropped in for the sharks. This person feigned dead with minor bullet injury swam ashore an uninhabited island and finally rescued after the surrender of the Japanese forces. The other one related to a horrific incident about 54 Indian prisoners taken by the Japanese in a lorry, shot from point blank range and interned in a mass grave at Wimberlygunj, 15 kilometers from the capital town of Port Blair. The story of heroic resistance including various failed attempts to escape from the Cellular jail was hair-splitting in its intensity.

Reminiscing about those tortuous and gloomy days they could also recollect some romances involving the earliest prisoners some of whom after completing their prison terms came out, had some romantic dalliance, married locally and settled on the island town. That was the indomitable proverbial human spirit. We met some members of families whose ancestors had been incarcerated in Port Blair during the late 19th and early 20th centuries. We were told of early efforts to grow vegetables and fruits despite high salinity and thunderous torrential rains lasting more than six months. Then came the next best initiative to start school education at Port Blair for the offspring of settlers. Thus despite extreme hardships, deprivations, tortures and even high rates of morbidity and mortality, the determined human will could not be suppressed. By indulgence in newer vocations many started finding the meaning of life in their new abode of inhospitable climes.

B.R. Ambedkar said, *"I feel that the constitution is workable, it is flexible and it is strong enough to hold the country together both in peacetime and in wartime. Indeed, if I may say so, if things go wrong under the new Constitution, the reason will not be that we had a bad Constitution. What we will have to say is that Man was vile.*" I am also reminded of a beautiful line I read somewhere about the Republic Day, "Freedom in mind, faith in words, pride in our hearts and memories in our souls" – a very nice statement of rational and clear thinking about a solemn occasion like this. Viewed in the above context, what follows was an eye-opener.

On our repeated query about the distinction between the 'then administration' and the 'present bureaucracy', we were left shame-faced and worried about the image of the existing administrative infrastructure in the country. To our consternation the comments were not flattering. The freedom fighters felt that the quality of governance had gone down drastically; that the bureaucracy was much more efficient during the British rule as also more fair and honest then. The respect and awe with which some ICS officers were talked about did not compare favourably with their today's counterparts. The freedom fighters did not mince words in pointing out that there was much corruption in administration 'now'. Some put the final nail in the coffin by opting, given a chance, to go back to the British system of governance rather than the 'present' dispensation. That was a sad commentary on our administrative culture and organization, and we could not stop ourselves from reflecting, where we had gone wrong.

Nation- Building – Creating Landmarks and Preserving the Heritage

Making of a Nation passes through long and arduous stages. It takes shape with shared collective identity, consciousness and cultural affinity over centuries, an underlying idea of being akin and distinct from people of another geographic confine. There are also physical markers of a nation that distinguish it from another landmass and assign it pride with reference to the 'other'. These may also get associated with nature's bounty like the Himalayas, the Niagara Falls, the Grand Canyon, the Great Barrier Reef, the Ganga or man-made wonders of the world such as the Taj Mahal, the Acropolis, the Colosseum, the Eiffel Tower, the Pyramids etc. to name a few. These cultural icons of those societies endorse the feeling of oneness and bind their communities together. Countries build monuments, memorials, parliament houses, stadia, national parks and museums, and evolve literature, art, dance and music that all go to reinforce and buttress the notion of one land. All these are venerated and preserved as natural and cultural heritage by mature nationalities.

It is therefore, time to evaluate - moments when one needs to pause and ponder - what have been the gains and where one is heading to. Before preservation, we may first talk of creation. The ancient Indians built grand Angkorwat, Parambanan and Borobudur temples and many more beyond the boundaries of India, and some in down south like Brihadeshwara temple. But there are no monuments or structures built in modern India that may really be boasted about. This inadequacy should not be explained away by citing economic reasons as State always has enough resources to splurge. When it is done for a good cause and for public purpose, no one complains. The failure has been occasioned more by lack of vision and absence of a national passion to 'build'. In the process we forgot to honour our freedom fighters and the unsung heroes.

In retrospect, one may say that Independent India ought to have celebrated the end of British colonialism by raising a colossus as tribute to the Idea of India, to the yearning of freedom, to the sacrifices of countless unsung heroes who fought for independence, and for celebrating the eventual attainment of freedom. It would have added to the national pride and given an iconic symbol to the youth. Holding ceremonies at India Gate and Gateway of India – essentially symbols of British supremacy and show of splendour by the British before a subjugated nation – for paying tribute is a compromise and not an originality. The statement is not meant to undermine the social and architectural value of these edifices, they are imposing and beautiful. It is also not intended to diminish many administrative, social and political gains attained through the British rule in India. But it is to highlight the irony that we did not create our own body of art to honour the martyrs of the first war of independence (1857) or for remembering tens of thousands of Indians who perished over the next century following 1857 Rising and through the freedom struggle. Lest we miss, or for some blissful ignorant men and women, these monuments were built to commemorate British successes, and as an incidental memorial adjunct to the Indian soldiers who laid down their life overseas in the service of the colonial paymasters for their colonial interests.

A similar apathy is visible in the matter of preserving our cultural and architectural heritage. Excepting the Hindi/regional films that are doing fine, Indian folk traditions, music and dances do not occupy position of pride but are only relied upon for rhetorical appreciation during official functions. However, more disturbing is our neglect of the architectural heritage. They cry for attention bearing shabby looks and stand vandalised. They are difficult to access, unkempt and filthy, mostly in decrepit surroundings and overseen by an unenthusiastic set of government employees who never smile. While most heritage structures are encroached, altered, and desecrated, others are either destroyed or are on the verge of destruction. Those that exist are grossly undervalued due to negligence. Maintenance and upkeep of all such spaces is the most neglected area of governance. There is equal lack of awareness on the part of the citizens and the keepers. The commitment to preserve the national heritage is missing because its value as cultural asset is not recognised.

There are government bodies responsible for such tasks but their functionaries are not mentally and intellectually attuned to the important task in their hands. An appropriate orientation needs to be inculcated in them to make them proficient with the job as also to enkindle love for it; a point that needs very special attention during the selection process and later for imparting training. The public also needs to be sensitised through well-designed information education campaign to contribute in preserving and promoting the national cultural heritage.

A World Heritage Site, Goa

Linking Work Culture and Integrity with Nationalism

The theaters in Goa follow the wonderful practice of presenting the national anthem before the movie starts. Everyone gets up and joins the choir with light humming that adds to the serenity and the beauty of the anthem. We are not treated to this feast for the soul in movie halls in many other parts of the country and therefore Goa takes the cake. It gets the distinction even though it achieved freedom from the Portuguese rule much later and joined the Indian Union only in 1961. We know that the national anthem had moved the freedom fighters who showed rare courage and determination in their struggles against the might of the British Empire. Love and respect for the national flag is a universal phenomenon and must be encouraged in the youth.

The feeling of nationalism is one of the unique characteristics of human beings that make them proud of shared consciousness, common heritage and cultural identity. It is an affirmative trait much revered the world over. Great fates have been achieved by people inspired by nationalism and the highest sacrifices were also made by people who were driven by nationalistic urges. Reimagining the place of nationalism in the life of ordinary citizens and more so for children in schools and colleges might help in creating a cadre of committed men and women for future good governance and ethical administration.

What happened to the Scouts and Guides Movement and passion for NCC in our youth? These institutions have dwindled and lost value in the madness of consumerist culture. We can reorient the younger generation towards nationalistic fervor by reviving these institutions and recapitulating the heroics of freedom fighters who made the greatest sacrifices for the sake of the motherland. Linking this with the performance of government servants may be considered through appropriate training programs.

Promoting integrity and efficient work culture has been the most daunting task in public administration. It is unfortunate that the country ranks at the lowest rung on corruption in the world. From the moneys stashed in the Swiss Banks to various financial and land scams, there is a long list of corrupt practices bringing bad name to the country. The other aspect much talked about is the so called "policy paralysis". The development programs get stalled owing to the twin problem of corruption and inefficiency. The divide between the urban and rural population, the rich and the poor, the strong and the weak and the educated and the uneducated keeps widening as a direct consequence of this malfeasance.

There may be many prescriptions for stemming the rot as there could be many ways of tackling a given problem. It is suggested that a good result may come from relying and propagating nationalistic feelings among the people through a healthy and positive outlook. We may try to address the twin dilemma of corruption and inefficiency through the medium of nationalism. The objective should be to unleash positive energy of the community through nationalistic fervor and channelize it for creative work of increasing efficiency and shunning corruption.

Having pride about once country and its cultural heritage is an excellent thing; the opposite of it is inferiority complex. Pride can come through goodness and sense of achievement. The stories of scams and frauds do us no good, neither the proverbial stupor of the State machinery. Therefore pride in the country will be more when the brighter side appears distinct. For achieving the brighter side one has to constantly polish the surface; in other words, conscious efforts to excel and innovate. This in a way would be a positive cycle of action and reaction. Attainment of success and resultant pride are thus closely related and mutually complimentary. Early school education must have emphasis on this aspect of character building through interesting curriculum but rigorous training where the teacher and pupil must regularly interact. There is no magic wand to reach the destination. But a beginning can be made and earlier the better.

Time to have an Indian Link Language

English continues to be the only Pan India language that acts as the link for most of our countrymen to converse with each other. From cultural exchange to trade and commerce, from corporate functioning to government communications, the dependence on English is all pervasive. Bill boards, media advertising, signage and even advice 'not to spit' and 'do not litter' are found written in English. So we seem to be totally overawed by this foreign language and enamored by its versatile reach and power. So far so good! But is it good for our national pride? Haven't all non-English speaking countries developed without the dependence on a borrowed language? After 66 years of independence, the sole reliance on the language of our erstwhile rulers does no credit to the political and administrative classes of the country.

English indeed is a very rich and useful language that is spoken in large parts of the world, including by a large number of expatriate Indians. Indians' command over this language is admired and many Indian writers regularly produce international best-sellers. Many professors and scientists rely on English to teach and research in the best universities of the world. The efficacy and usefulness of English is not the issue as an instrument of communication with the outside world, higher learning, researches etc. The only question that begs explanation is why the growth of a national language for inland communication has remained asymmetrical. Appallingly we have not been able to substitute an Indian language for all-India communication all these years – dependence on English has only increased.

Globalization need not be decried for sway of English; utility of the language for the global market is a good enough reason for it to be learnt and mastered as a medium of international communication. But why should we need it for dealing in a typical Indian market. Any two 'well-educated' Indians, not known to each other will invariably begin the conversation in English because they do not have the self-confidence to start talking in an Indian language lest their status gets diminished. Two strangers, each humming a Bollywood song would find it normal to ask for direction or time in English, one form the other. If it is not low esteem, then what it is? From a passenger sitting next to you in a flight, or a bell boy in the hotel, or a cricket or tennis star, our conversation request would always be in English.

No Chinese, Korean, Japanese, Russian, French, Italian, German or Spanish man or woman suffers from such inhibitions or feels so insecure talking in his/her mother tongue like we do.

A fall-out of this lop-sided language policy or the lack of it is that the new generation does not have a good knowledge of any Indian language. And his/her command over English is often limited, being a foreign language. The end result is that more and more people are not able to speak or write any language with ease and reassurance. It seems our collective consciousness to have a lingua-franca is facing inertness. Experts opine that children's learning ability enhances in their mother tongue because that is the language in which they think. But in our quest for everything English we have totally ignored this fair principle and adopted a language, which is alien to Indian's psyche and emotional being. The result is that more and more of our countrymen are not good in their mother tongue and converse imperfectly in a language that does not belong to them.

The knowledge of English definitely helps in finding better jobs as it elevates its protagonist to a higher level. But once good at it they start looking down upon those who do not speak the language. It has created a divide in the society between the affluent and the powerful who express themselves in English and those who cannot. This attitude has grown from a deep sense of inferiority in relation to the Western culture, and English being the headiest symbol of that culture provides a magical spell.

We did not plan well for a link language. We did not prioritize the need to evolve an acceptable language early on that could replace English in say fifteen-twenty years after independence. All Indian languages have suffered because of the lack of this clarity and resolve. Considering the overall reach and number, Hindi could have evolved over the years as the natural medium of national communication and therefore the pan-Indian lingua-franca. But we did not do our homework well. The antagonism had a historical context, which could be addressed by statesmanship and judicious application of a forward language policy. The lack of it resulted in the failure of the so-called three language formula as nobody seems to know more than two languages in this country. Our government welfare programs are notified in English for a population that does not understand it. Typically most work in government offices and trials in courts are conducted and orders issued in words that are Latin to the puzzled petitioners. They sign on trust, affidavits in courts and documents in government offices that are 'read over' to them by their benefactors. The largest democracy ought to do better than this.

**The National Flag, Connaught Place, New Delhi -
the Epitome of Indian Nationalism**

Indian Militants of 20th Century were Different

We revere our revolutionaries, branded then as terrorists by the British because they took to arms to defend the honor of our country. Rightly so, they are now our venerated freedom fighters and martyrs who laid down their lives for the better future of our country. They raised the wounded pride of their motherland at a time when she was undergoing humiliating subjugation by foreign imperialists. We may recall how a reign of terror was unleashed in Punjab by the British in the aftermath of Jallianwala Bagh Massacre and how people in Amritsar were asked to crawl on their four limbs before the cheering British forces. We also know how the subsequent British Inquiry left the perpetrator of that crime against humanity, Brig. Edward Dwyer with patronizing reprimand. Even before this, the shameful *KomagataMaru* episode had happened involving wanton police killing of Indian workers at Calcutta (now Kolkata), hundred years before the date of writing of this piece, i.e. 27th September 1914.

The then Lt. Governor of Punjab, Michael O' Dwyer was later shot dead by revolutionary Udham Singh in London in 1940. While such reprisals appeared then to many people as unacceptable, there is no denying the fact that incidents like this would have enkindled the fire in the hearts of Indians then and does it so when we read about their selfless heroics. We cannot forget the martyrdom of Bhagat Sigh, Rajguru, Sukhdev, Bismil, Ashfaqullah and several others who laid down their lives at the altar of freedom – they were household names in India, woven in folklores and stories for young children – but branded then as traitors by the British regime.

Similarly Mukti Bahini and African National Congress volunteers were seen as law-breakers in the eyes of their governments but as heroes by their suffering countrymen. That would be the scenario for most freedom fighters of suppressed nationalities who had struggled to rid themselves free from the colonial masters. Even PLO under Yasser Arafat, despite being a kind of militant outfit was generally considered to be freedom fighters, so much so, that it was recognized among others by the Government of India.

However, these individuals and groups belonged to a different genre – persons like them are not made any more. Their commitment, loyalty and sacrifice were of a very high order; their stories so inspiring. It is difficult to fathom the depth of their love for their motherland. And they seldom caused harm to innocent people. Now we have the new breed of militants who are rightly identified as terrorists by the world at large. They spare no innocents, not even women and children. It might perhaps sound harsh but they truly have no religion or code of conduct whatsoever. No organized religion permits such bloodletting.

The so-called 'Islamists' of various hues, Al Qaida et al and their latest avatar, Islamic State are indulging in worst un-Islamic crimes that can be. Flushed with ill-gotten petro-dollars, equipped by greedy arms suppliers and seeped in ignorance, they present the saddest spectacle of everything that Islam does not stand for. Islam means peace and Allah is always invoked in all the verses of Quran as 'the most benevolent and merciful'. So they cannot carry out such vicious killings in the name of Allah. If anything, they are only as much Muslim, as were Hitler, Franco and Mussolini Christian, with the exception that these ruthless latter despots did not raise the war cry in the name of Christianity. Ironically the terrorists operating in many parts of the Muslim world are killing more Muslims, for whose welfare they profess to commit these horrendous crimes, than non-Muslims and that too in the name of Islam; that is the most tragic contradiction of the situation. Apart from the ethical and religious angles and moral repugnancy of attack on innocent persons, there is another cogent reason why such activities cannot be condoned by any flexible interpretations, even as we leave reference to Vienna Convention and violation of Human Rights as defined in UN Charters.

Unlike the first-mentioned erstwhile groups, later ones like the Tamil militants in Sri Lanka, our own Punjab militants in 1980s, the Left-wing militants then and now, the 'Islamist' militants of today – there is nothing Islamic about them, except the visible beards – are mostly fighting against democratically elected or legally appointed governments. These militant groups had/have the option to join the political spectrum, work around it and gain strength to push through the change they want to see in the policies and programs. But they pugnaciously work against the system instead of working around the given political structure, at huge cost both to themselves and others. This democratic option was no way available to our venerated militants of early 20th century India and that too puts them totally apart from these assorted varieties.

Thus by first doggedly refusing to be within the existing political gamut and then attacking its institutions, most of the present age militants do not come out with clean hands. Working against a military regime, an autocracy or a repressive regime is one thing – not that, resort to violence is condonable by any such delineation – but not relying on available alternative resource in a democratic regime and frequently trying to subvert it with violence shows that such elements have no commitment to the professed objectives, rather they clearly have other hidden agenda or worse sometimes, play a proxy war on behalf of one or the other power.

Cultural Renaissance Sans Divisiveness

Mark Twain is credited with this remarkable statement, *"India is the cradle of the human race, the birthplace of human speech, the mother of history, the grandmother of legend, and the great grandmother of tradition. Our most valuable and most instructive materials in the history of man are treasured up in India only"*. How flattering! India's syncretic treasure has much to be desired and can be reverentially redistributed without the fear of it ever getting depleted. That confidence is unfortunately getting shaken in many ways. In the cacophony of discordant voices, saner rumblings are getting drowned. The challenge to save those reverberations should be a cardinal democratic endeavor, more so when the discordance has strong ideological under-pinning and supported strongly by determined forces. Ownership and declaratory assertions of nationalism are positive traits, until used as subterfuge to attack others. The response therefore has to carry equal conviction and ideally seen to be attempting to address those concerns, albeit with more positive vibrations.

Nationhood has several elements; preservation and promotion of its built heritage may be construed to be one of these that can generate pride and give a constructive diversion. Not surprising that Walt Disney observed, *"Our heritage and ideals, our code and standards – the things we live by and teach our children – are preserved or diminished by how freely we exchange ideas and feelings".* Let us be more mindful of convergence points and focus on a neglected area of our national culture as reflected through heritage sites.

The Heritage Sites are valued and revered the world over. Many parts of the world have heritage sites in multiple cities, which they have taken care to preserve, maintain and present aesthetically to the visitors. A visit to the heritage sites is a huge attraction for international tourists who often include this item at the top of their itinerary in India. We are endowed with beautiful monuments, dotted all over the country and spread over various states. We also have the strength of a very old civilization resplendent with rich tradition, diverse cultures, geographical expanse, natural beauties, and wildlife. It is therefore surprising that the number of tourists visiting our country is perhaps less than the number that visits the tiny city state of Singapore in a year. Of course, there are structural, administrative and systemic deficiencies in our policies, and the way we do things, which inhibit a thriving tourist culture in our country. But coming to specifics, tourist would feel less threatened if the spaces are accessible, walk able, safe and free from nuisance.

Limiting our present discussion to heritage sites as one of the major elements of tourist attraction, we may try to identify the causes behind the missing number. We need to appreciate that showcasing a site, like packaging and presentation of merchandise, is an integral strategy of marketing. The same applies to our tourist destinations. Regrettably we have slackness, inefficiency, corruption and suffer from lack of imagination. The inelasticity of the policy and its tardy execution is too apparent to be explained at length, notwithstanding some imaginative campaigns like the Incredible India.

A public policy has to be guided by a vision, a set of objectives, and the methodology to attain these, followed by periodic evaluation of the progress and backed up by regular up-gradation and mid-course correction. Our sites are poorly maintained, dirty and inaccessible. We must begin by providing the ease of access - the heritage sites are not always well connected by public transport. Even where they are, they do not provide a good walking experience in and around the monument due to poorly-kept or non-existent pavements, rubble and litter strewn all over, dimly-lit walkways etc. The heritage sites have to be well-sanitized with complete ease of walking around without being bothered by any nuisance. The visitor should be able to enjoy the aesthetics and serenity of the place. He/she should get an enabling environment to be transported to that era which is being visited – that ambience has to be created – so that the person takes home a totality of the experience of the place.

The surroundings of the heritage sites should be artistically laid out, making them pleasant to the senses; they must beckon the visitors to visit them on their own. A decent friendly reception area at heritage sites where visitors feel welcome is a must. What we have instead, is a gloomy, inhospitable, and ramshackle structure with rusted iron grills on its windows and some tired, unsmiling, irritable person behind the counter who spreads no cheer either. So apart from aesthetics, the whole culture of treating the visitors needs to undergo a transformation. We must improve the environs of our heritage sites and put only those on job who know how to smile and have an aptitude for such calling. This requires education and training from early age. This may be summed up by quoting British historian, Niall Ferguson, *"What makes a civilization real to its inhabitants, in the end, is not just the splendid edifice at its center, nor even the smooth functioning of the institutions they house. At its core, a civilization is the texts that are taught in its schools, learned by its students and recollected in times of tribulation".*

Having a Sense of History

It is good to have a sense of history. It is almost a clichéd saying that those who forget history are condemned to live by it. In other words, there are important lessons to be learnt from history. There have been leaders in every country who had shown a sense of history that reflected in their actions. One comes across many persons with humble beginning who later became big and prominent in their respective fields but worked and acted in a way that showed them to have had a sense of history. We have a very rich history. Ours is one of the oldest civilisations of the world. Our country has been the cradle of a rich and varied culture with remarkable past achievements of art and craft, poetry and literature, dance, drama and music, architecture and sculptor etc., which are all unparalleled except perhaps some likeness with other ancient civilisations of Egypt and Mesopotamia.

It is in this context that the lack of vision for the future appears to be rather disconcerting. Preservation of legacy and heritage should have been the core of our cultural inheritance. Alas, that is not the case. Taking just one example of architecture, the achievement of the countrymen in the ancient times especially with reference to religious structures is unparalleled. But it does not have any comparison to the architecture of the modern era. We have not made serious efforts to preserve our architectural heritage; the same is victim of vandalism mostly. On the other hand, the growth of a utilitarian, contemporary, yet aesthetically chic class of architecture has also eluded us.

The quest to find a place in history should actually be a universal longing. That is how it is in a well rounded society. Thus, this yearning could be at the national level, in a particular region, a particular place or district, a village, an institution, a college or school, a club or a society - in any organisation or even in an individual. It could also be with a group of persons, a family, a professional class etc. There are instances where an institution/organisation/ individual is found following precepts and practices that betray a clearly developed sense of history. This would be necessarily a conscious effort but something gradually ingrained as these entities grew on. Carrying forward the inherited legacy becomes a tradition which perhaps is a function of historical sense.

The Taj Hotel in Mumbai was in news recently having passed through the painful anniversary of a brutal attack 6 years ago. It is admirable that having gone through such an ordeal, the icon has moved on with pride and confidence. The inside and outside of the hotel again shows the great sense of history possessed by its founders. It is not surprising that the family that created the structure is still thriving and is recognised for their various achievements. Can the same be said about a newer structure in the city which despite its 27 storeys does not inspire such adulation nor would perhaps elicit great admiration in the distant future?

Many of our towns and cities today unfortunately cannot boast of historical buildings or institutions. Most old institutions and structures have been obliterated or are getting pulled down by the new owners. This is as much for money as due to the lack of appreciation and concern for history. Partnerships have collapsed, joint ventures have disappeared and joint families have disintegrated in the face of stiff competition, rivalries and lust for fast money. Many of the traditional art and crafts have vanished as successive generations have veered away from the profession of their forefathers but the economic reason behind such departure is a reality and has to be given due regard. The cost of real estate having gone sky rocketing, it is actually not appropriate to find faults with the people who try to sway with times and get enriched. The legitimate expectation of enrichment and attaining material prosperity, therefore, cannot be decried.

What however we may earnestly try to figure out is whether economic progress and prosperity necessarily means putting history into the dustbin. The answer to this should be a clear no. The desire for mullah would be no less strong among sections of people inhabiting the rich parts of the worlds. However, they belong to cities that have preserved heritage pockets and upgraded them with great care and concern. And their maintenance is done by professionals with a sense of duty, with the willing and enthusiastic contribution of the local inhabitants. This concern, involvement, desire and efforts in that direction are missing as much as a cultural trait as from the State policy.

One example of this missing trait can be readily cited by the fact that we do not cherish much the memories of the departed. How else should we explain the absence of memorials for the brave-hearts who sacrificed their lives for the freedom of the country? We must not confuse this with the memorials of the national leaders which are preserved with pomp and glory. The ordinary mortals and the humble soldiers on the other hand, who died fighting for country's freedom, have largely remained unrecognised. We must need to think why structures like India Gate and Gateway of India have not been built by us since independence. Unless we remember and idolise our national un-sung heroes of the past, how would the future remember us for whatever worth we are.

OBSERVATION
OUT THERE

Destruction and a New Life, An earthquake-ravaged hospital in Bhuj

The World That Was

From 'The Third Wave' to 'Future Shock' to 'The World is Flat', there have been innumerable books that have commented upon technology's swift drive in the fast lane that is leaving the world ill equipped to keep pace with the radical transformation, especially where change is the only constant. One is reminded of that prophetic poet, Mirza Ghalib who wrote in the middle of the 19th century, "… *Rau me hai rakhsh-e-umar, kahaan dekhiye thame/ne haath baag par hai, na paa hai rakab me*"! (the horse of the era is galloping, see where it stops/neither the hands are in control of the reins, nor the foot are holding the stirrups). And Ghalib had the right credentials to use the metaphor as may be deduced from his yet another couplet about himself, "*sau pusht se hai pesha-e-aaba sipahgiri/kuch shayari hi zariya-e-izzat nahi mujhe*"!(for centuries my ancestors have been trained archers/it is not the writing of poetry alone that brings laurels to me). Digression apart, what a philosophical exposition of an era that appeared to Ghalib's discerning eyes at the verge of rapid obliteration when all familiar symbols from the past were getting wiped out from the vision and minds. Some amongst the bewildered lot would desperately cling on to the timeworn order in the hope that the storm would subside and they would be able to follow once again the older ways of life and continue with their existence at the old pace. Though it was not to be became clear subsequently.

Nobody should be faulted if occasional nostalgia grips some of us with reference to olden times, especially memories of certain events, places, things or elements. It is more pronounced because transformation in culture and technology has been unprecedented during the last two decades. It is roughly the period, during which a generational change occurs, thereby making such a wide difference in experience and perception of people that facts give the impression of being myths. Many instances and illustrations can be given to substantiate the radical difference between what used to be and what is there now.

An interesting reference may be made to the hostel life when dependence on Money Order was near total – it used to be with great expectation and jubilation as guys returned for lunch and gathered around the postman, in fact message would flash in advance as one dropped from the bus and started heading to the hostel. It is inconceivable that the joy of getting the much-awaited cash delivered in your hands can ever be matched by the withdrawal of currency from the ATMs – as the hostellers invariably do now – the lurking awareness pervading that the balance would diminish.

Train reservation was another area with lot of excitement as one would travel to station and the clerk would open a massive register the size of a table to pass his benefaction with or without consideration from behind a grilled window. How so ever you might try you could never reach his collars, the man securely perched at a high chair when he disdainfully announced that there was no vacancy – a one way communication – the berth most likely going to the next in line whose blinks and hints were pregnant with meaning. Now all that can be done today at the click of a mouse. There is neither allure for the clerk nor charm for the other party as standing in a queue sometimes shaped romantic possibilities.

How can one forget that massive black contraption called telephone – remember that black heavy appliance - which only worked by rolling the device with your right finger several times over? It was so romantic watching Sadhna or Nutan working on that machine and dialing it with their long fingers, trying to demurely convey a message for the evening rendezvous to the person at the other end, overlooking their shoulders lest somebody from the family hears that clicking sound. Alas that practice has irretrievably passed on to a bygone era! Another interesting aspect was that the telephone could be found only at some appointed place of the house – even the cordless had not yet arrived – so that you just could not hide from the preying eyes or poking noses of the elders while talking. The mobile now could take you anywhere, what a contrast!

Another remarkable process during the bygone era was making the outstation calls. By the time your call materialized it would be another day, and in any case the entire neighbourhood would know of your labour as one had to scream at the pitch of one's voice in letting the other person hear what one was trying to say. It would disconnect several times and the helpful operator would yell back at you to continue. The conversation would be like a verbal fight between two persons, both shouting at the pitch of their voice.

Bill for this non-conversation could be as high as Rs.80-100 then. What a fun it was? What terrible loss to have missed such processes to the marauding race of unfeeling times! We are devoid of that amusement only because this little thing 'cell', as small as the name itself has intruded into our life so obtrusively that even the wash room is not private any more. There are occasions when family members rush to the toilet door for reassurance that it is just a conversation and that nothing is amiss with the incumbent of the hot seat.

The black era TV was known in our homes through *DoordarshanSamachar* (TV News) and *krishidarshan* (Agri show). The highlight was *chitrahaar* (film songs), being the ultimate prize a family could get for free from the national broadcaster. The array of programs available today is mind-boggling. The channels have altered our life forever, delivering unlimited entertainment, wholesome or not, one does not know. We know about the couch potatoes and the resultant increase of human radius and diameter. The internet completes the picture of individual's isolation from the rest of his surrounding as he remains glued to the whole world except his own near and dear ones under the same roof. The quest is for social networking with impersonal beings ignoring those who are at home, in the neighborhood or the community. As we chase the mirage mindlessly, only time will tell how good or bad this alienation with the more tangible and accessible world was.

In the old world, community was more important; there was less emphasis on individual pursuits. Entertainment meant going on picnic with family and cousins, playing outdoor, kite flying, kabaddi, cricket and football. That promoted lot of camaraderie, sportsmanship, community-mindedness and was a learning experience for the youngsters.

Films have been very popular in Indian social milieu. They represent and reflect the hopes & despairs, aspirations, joys & fears and more so the culture, fashion and love life of the times. The era of coy courtship is past; it is now more volatile and 'live in' is cool. The ultimate change may be portrayed by citing the song sequence on Madhubala, *'zidagi bhar nahi hulegi wo barsaat ki raat'* as the height of romanticism with its exquisitely magical spell; now we hear *'bidi jalaile jigar se piya, jigar ma badi aag hai'* or *'munni badnaam hui'* or *'sheila ki jawaani'* (opening lines of a Hindi film song then and some Hindi film songs now).

A Society without Hatred
is a Tall Order

Hate is a powerful emotion. It has driven people to great heights err... depths! Serious crimes of passion are committed by people, overpowered by hatred. The great Bard of classic English literature, William Shakespeare is credited with these words, *"love me or hate me, both are in my favour....if you love me, I'll always be in your heart...if you hate me, I'll always be in your mind"*! That means, pretty huge sum of time and energy is wasted in nurturing deleterious feelings that do no good to its possessor but keep him/her preoccupied with the thoughts of the person who is the recipient of their resentment. Sadly neither natural disasters nor wild animals have done so much harm to humanity as humans themselves. From ancient times to the beginning of 21st century, worst offences have been perpetrated by man against man. Animals do not attack each other in hatred but because of hunger or fear. Humans alone have this unique distinction of causing harm to their own breed even without any provocation and the saving grace is that this distinction more squarely rests on the doors of men as women have rarely engaged in organized wrong-doings or incidents of mass violence.

Hostility and intolerance create a disabling social environment and naturally the products of that environment exhibit that legacy. But let us have a different take on this grotesque human attribute. Shall we say that economic disparity and inequality leading to distress cause resentment, heart-burns, revulsion and anger that perhaps lead to many social crimes? The existence of gated communities and ghettoization of human settlements is an indicator of tensions within the cities. There may be communal or caste-based identities fanning such trends to some extent but the root cause is the inequitable distribution of nation's resources and deprivations that are largely perceived as the direct result of machinations by powerful moneyed people. Nothing is more irksome than exploitation.

The inadequacy, powerlessness, subjection to apparent injustice and the resultant frustration become a breeding ground for antipathy that erupts at the slightest trigger of social upheaval. Many intense reactions the world over are exhibited by sections of people, who were tormented by denial of entitlements or who perceived themselves as the victims of injustices, and the outbursts may sit at an emotive tinder-box. It must however be stated clearly that it is not at all a suggestion that poor are prone to commit offences because they are the aggrieved lot. Left to themselves they are more law-abiding than the rich, and they have more empathy. But it is the realization of relative adversity and painful comparisons that kindle resentment. This feeling of being denied the due because the system is corrupt, inefficient, unresponsive, and heavily balanced against the weak and the poor, reinforces the perceived or real grievances, aggravating the social tensions.

Greed and mindless conspicuous consumption perpetuate the contrast between the rich and the poor; already different centuries coexist in our country, from bullock cart to Lamborghini. Consumerism at its height may be commercially profitable but it has a huge social cost, which gets further exasperated as the enlarging economy is not found to be an enabler by the disadvantaged sections to seek any such indulgence. Those who are left behind are losing their patience and it has to be a matter of serious concern for the planners. Urban sprawls cannot be safe havens without catering to the rightful aspirations of multitudes that play their role in the economic activities that sustain the comfort levels of better-offs.

Generation of wealth is a prerequisite for the country to grow beyond the tag of emerging economy. But that also means affording opportunity to the youth to get some reward of his hard work, to realize his potential and above all experience some sensitivity in the system, which is willing to take him along. Platitudes and freebees would increasingly be inadequate to address this issue. The public policies have to foster them and include them through sustainable developmental planning. The feeling of neglect and injustice cannot be eradicated by cosmetic sweet-nothingness. Real growth would happen only through strong commitments. It should also be considered a matter of self-preservation for the rising middle classes; alone they cannot move without the peril of serious fall-outs.

A sensitive poet like Sahir penned his gut-wrenching poem, *'jinhe naaz hai Hind pe vo kahaan hain'!*(where are those who are proud of India) and more disturbingly in these lines, *"Sansaar kee har ek besharmi, ghurbat kee gode me palti hai//chaklon me hee aakar rukti hai, faqon me joraah nikalti hai"!* (all the stories of shame emanate from poverty/starvations lead nowhere but to brothels). The pride in our country and the Idea of India is incomplete without an inclusive agenda that moves beyond the clichés of disguised doles. Though a scientist, Einstein made a social science statement when he said, *"Imagination is everything. It is the preview of life's coming attractions."* We need a visualizer who can imagine and build an India of our dreams.

Human Migration
– Story of Incredible Courage

Interests and perspectives vary widely – a huge gap when it is between the winner and the vanquished. It could not be more revealing than in recalling the forced transfers of human population that happened in large numbers from time to time. The main context is the world colonialism that was at its peak during the 18th and 19th centuries. Huge transfers of population routinely took place from one corner of the globe to another including establishment of penal settlements in far flung colonies by the imperialist powers. From Africa to the West Indies to the smaller territories of Fiji, Surinam, Maldives and many others, very few parts of the world remained untouched by this trans-continental human movement. One of the earliest was of course the English settlement in North America from 1607 onward that continued for close to two hundred years and culminated in the American War of Independence in 1776. This necessitated finding new regions of penal settlement as well as trading centers as per the time-tested policy of the colonialists.

The first arrival in Australia was in 1788, popularly known as the First Fleet comprising eleven ships carrying around one thousand persons including around seven hundred prisoners. That occasion is celebrated by a large population in Australia as a remarkable fate of man's adventurous spirit. But it is also referred to as the Invasion Day by the Aborigines of Australia. The

English settlements started growing in New Zealand around the same period. The earliest arrival of Indian convicts and others in our own Andaman Islands was in 1858 soon after the suppression of the first War of Independence.

The history of modern Australia is therefore as recent as just over two centuries, in sharp contrast to our own almost three thousand years of cultural continuity and yet sadly with such huge gap in the levels of development of the two nations. The First Fleet that left Great Britain in May 1787 arrived eight months later and 48 persons less (deaths during the voyage) to what was called New South Wales to establish the first European colony in Australia. There was no looking back and what we have today is one of the most thriving urban conglomerates in the world. The American dream is yet another story of grand success that initially started as a penal colony. Our humbler Port Blair as the capital and the main town of Andaman has also developed into a neat and tidy trading and administrative township of modest size but with good tourist potential. It abounds in natural and scenic beauty, salubrious landscape, corals, and lagoons with glorious view of the Bay of Bengal all around.

But there is also the poignant and grave history of human sufferings at the penal settlement in Andaman that eventually gave way to the dreaded Cellular Jail, notorious for its tortuous incarceration of prisoners hundreds of miles away from their near and dear ones. And many of these were not criminals but political activists who were exiled to the *Kaalapani*(dark waters) by the British with the dual intention of keeping them segregated from the other freedom fighters in the mainland and to send the message that similar fate awaited those who dared to contest the British might. The first voyage that touched its shore in March 1858 with prisoners and others had suffered many casualties before landing and many more soon after disembarkation. The living conditions for the Indians were extremely difficult with unhealthy climate, humidity, presence of large number of pests and snakes, unhygienic and frugal quantity of food, murky drinking water, non-existent medical facilities and inadequate clothing and shelter.

It is almost impossible today to visualise what went on in the daily lives of these prisoners and their Indian supervisors. Punishment for the slightest protest was meted with unmitigated cruelty. Raising any voice against the atrocities amounted to challenging the authority and therefore a rebellious behaviour and a jail offence, inviting further reprisals. The mortality rate in the island was very high and equally so in the prison. No wonder that the relatives of those sent to *Kaalapani* presumed them dead with no hope of them ever returning alive. Mostly this proved true and large number of people died there itself unwept and unsung – many of these had struggled back home for the freedom of our country.

In the more recent past also owing to the two World Wars, the repressive policies of the Nazi and Fascist regimes, the vivisection of the Indian subcontinent, the Bosnian and Jordanian crisis and the hugely battle ravaged Iraq-Syria-Afghanistan sector, large populations have moved out of their homes in great distress.

While all this has been going on, there is a silver lining as well. The indomitable human will triumphed over these adversarial conditions, as from America to Australia to New Zealand to Andaman the settlers started trying to find new meaning to their life. They made exertions to reconstruct their life within those new and inhospitable environments. It is a tribute to those early settlers that these modern territories have become so developed and reckoned as places of importance that attract visitors from far and wide. Many generations later, the present inhabitants of these territories must gratefully remember their ancestors who made it possible for them, a century or two apart, to be socially and economically empowered communities in the countries of their adoption. We salute the indomitable human spirit that made it possible.

Think of Grey for Winning the Hearts

The primacy for our national goals should be social and economic renewal, to take the people beyond the grind of poverty and bring meaning and dignity in their lives. Unfortunately the parentheses – corruption, castism, and communalism create hurdles. If mind and consciousness brings out the best of human potentials, it also breeds the worst that begets sorrow, misery and pain. What is missed is that just as a good person, may do a wrong sometime, due to misjudgment or owing to circumstances, there may be a wrong-doing person who is not evil all the times.

What applies to an individual also applies to group of persons or a community. When it comes to demonizing the other person or group of persons, we generally tend to be opinionated and even condemnatory. The grey, which is the natural shade of human psyche, is generally shut off from our eyes. Absence of perception leads to grave errors of judgment and avoidable tragedies. Imperceptivity that breeds in mind gets translated into negativity and impacts harmony, social cohesion and inclusiveness. While compassion and empathy are not easy virtues, being perceptive may be a cultivated and learned trait. We may recall the words of Martin Luther King Jr, *"darkness cannot drive darkness; only light can do that; hate cannot drive out hate; only love can"*.

Democratic aspirations and commitments mean attainment of certain objectives for the entire population residing in a sovereign landmass, bounded by history, geography, social inter-dependence and shared consciousness of centuries. In the modern context, the objective boils down to creation of wealth – the ultimate mantra for a nation's progress and a marker of its having arrived. And how is that to be achieved? I read somewhere *'udyoginam purush singhmupaiti lakshmi'*, meaning that wealth loves to reside in the hands of an industrious person. Do we then have the time for squabbles and acrimony?

Prof. Rob Jenkins, commenting on the Indian political scenario lamented that instead of issue-oriented 'programmatic politics', Indian political system was mired in identity-based 'patronage politics'. The real worth and enterprise of the population is therefore getting checkmated due to shackles of mind. Equitable distribution of wealth through opportunities for the largest number is crucial. We cannot leave a sizable diffident population behind and feel safely ensconced, except at the cost of great peril. In times of upheavals, there is no guarantee of the safety of the gated habitations. Wellbeingness and belongingness cannot come without restoring dignity of the deprived sections.

A scares economy drives prizefight for the loaves and fishes and the resultant greediness and selfishness, perpetuate acquisitive desire. We know the glaring contrast presented by our urban centers – abject penurious living alongside crass opulence. Mindless acquisition and conspicuous consumption have become the hallmark of the upwardly mobile, unmindful of the reactions of the underprivileged sections and resentfulness of those who cannot afford. This seething bitterness of disadvantaged sections leads to volatility in temperament and vulnerability to emotive exploitation at the best of times.

Focusing on the task of nation-building may help in weaning people away from conflicting cognition. Cognition derived from ill-conceived or predisposed knowledge is dangerous and counter-productive. Right knowledge is as crucial for the building of an edifice as for the progression of a social formation. Along with dedicated efforts for economic development, we may, recognizing the cosmic principle of the underlying harmony of all faiths and people, strive to actualize that accord through synchronization of heads and hearts. Knowledge derived from understanding, perception, perspective and inter-faith dialogues would help in setting up a syncretic social mosaic. We may rely on the *AtharvaVeda* wherein it is said that 'love is the first born, loftier than the gods, fathers and men'. Bible declares, 'blessed are the merciful, as they shall obtain mercy'. Quran speaks of 'placing compassion and mercy in the hearts of those who follow Him'.

The way forward is to speak up – for those who have no or a weak voice. We cannot remain a bystander. We may remember what King Lear said to his daughter, *"Nothing will come out of nothing, speak again"!* In the din and cacophony of discordant rumblings, saner opinions must vouch for harmony. That alone will make the difference for the better. Pablo Picasso is said to have said, *"Others have seen what is and asked why. I have seen what could be and asked why not?"* That is the kind of intervention needed, to takes cudgels on behalf of the voiceless.

An illustration may be given from the exploits of an American 'social explorer'. In a real life story, 'The Kindness of Strangers - Penniless Across America' by Mike McIntyre, who ventured out of his well-endowed home and job, to travel across the country for one full year without any money, card, vehicle, contact or family; without begging or stealing either; he would offer to do some petty jobs in lieu of a night shelter or food. He survived and returned home after completing his quest for meaning of life. The key is therefore commonness and humaneness, underscoring distinctiveness, and thereby reach a stage where even a stranger is treated with kindness.

Reinterpreting and Imagining the Past

Comparisons are odious. That is more so when done with motives or intentions that are not so honourable. Drawing parallel from history comes in handy for various good and bad reasons. They serve purposes either way. However, as "those who forget history are condemned to live by it", there is advantage in taking positive lessons from history. But the problem is, we always try to interpret and narrate history as it suits us, resulting in misinterpretations, falsehood and calculated distortions. The pitfall arises because we externalise our own present experiences by projecting it in the past according to our predilections and prejudices. An attempt is therefore made here, not to rewrite history, not to provide alibi for various injustices of the past, but to flag one issue, namely looking at the past with a detached perspective.

The past social formations were not free from conflicts or strife. On the contrary, the maxim, 'might is right' was more widespread. Power literally flowed from the sword. There used to be constant violent struggles for power among the *shatraps*(war lords) and nobles that made life miserable for the common populace. Then there were adventurers and fortune seekers who wrought havoc wherever they went. But still the sectarian and communal divide was not so universal and wide spread as in modern times. The conflict was mainly militarist in nature, campaigns against adversaries, court intrigues and fratricidal wars among clansmen seeking the royal throne, and less to do with the common populace. It is this kind of framework that eludes our understanding and evaluation of the past.

The formal history writing that began under the British patronage, by singing eulogies for their 'Civilising Mission' and shouldering the 'Whiteman's Burden', tried to offer justification for the forced seizure of the country through deceit and war. That necessarily also meant writing disparagingly about every sphere of Indian past, and demonising the bygone era, making the contrast look much more glaring. Unfortunately, the same methodology in history writing continued to be followed by many Indian scholars of subsequent generations who took it upon themselves to twist the historical analyses further to align it with their respective predispositions. This projection of the modern-day consciousness (communalism) into the past was useful to posit particular political stance and gather support for the cause one was espousing. This positioning helped in promoting and facilitating both types of communalism in Colonial India.

Fact is that there was never any major communal conflagration in the pre-British India. Exceptions apart, the Turko-Afghan and Mughal rulers realised the impossibility of ruling the country without the support of the Indian ruling classes who were not their co-religionists. This trend became visible in the Delhi Sultanate and Mughal Empire where the ruling nobility had a wide ethnic spread and was drawn from various clans from the Central Asia and the Indian ruling classes. This was similarly followed in the Bahmani kingdom, or later the southern kingdoms of Mysore, Hyderabad etc. None of these can be called theological rules. They were neither claimed to be Islamic regimes by their own protagonists.

The monarchy in medieval India was essentially militarist which gradually learnt the statecraft – for examples, the theory of Kingship of Balban, Price Control Mechanism and huge standing army of Alauddin Khilji, shifting of capital and other measures of Muhammad Bin Tughlaq, administrative reforms of Sher Shah, *Sulh-e-kul* and *mansabdari* system of Akbar and several other things. Nowhere the historical records throw any evidence of medieval kings propagating any particular religion at the level of the state policy despite the nobility being predominantly Turko-Afghan and Mughal. The desecration of temples often emanated from the desire of declaring to the world the vanquishing of the 'enemy', typically a medieval war-cry. On the other hand there was a distinct non-Islamic flavour to the court etiquettes – non-Arabic in origin that was abhorrent to the more fundamentalist fringe – a deeply Persian influence. Even the sources of royal revenue were declared by some medieval religious scholars to be un-Islamic.

We had another vibrant intellectual strand, very catholic in its approach – the eclectic Sufi movement - which appealed to the masses irrespective of their religious beliefs and captured their imagination, and promoted understanding and tolerance for each other. Their discourses and narration were free from dogma. They laid emphasis on simplicity, charity, devotion and piety. The rich and the poor got equal treatment at these *khanqahs*(hermits) of Sufi saints. The teachings of Nizamuddin Aulia and the lyrics of Amir Khusro had huge mass appeal during their life time itself, and there were scores of Sufis and tens of hundreds of their followers from different faiths all over the country.

Two more points need special mention here: first, all these central Asian, Turkish and Afghan soldiers of fortune who occupied the throne of Delhi cumulatively for over six hundred years adopted this land as their home. With the exception of the founders of these dynasties, later rulers, especially of subsequent generations were born, lived and died in India, unlike from Metcalf and Clive to Dalhousie and Lord Mountbatten. Secondly, from 1707 when Aurangzeb died, to 1857 when the last Mughal was deposed, the Mughal rule had increasingly reduced in size and stature, practically confined to the Red Fort, but that did not stop the government from being run in his name. More significantly, despite there being many powerful king-makers, none of the successors to the throne during this long period of 150 years was anybody but a Mughal scion. That appears to be the conclusive social and political sanction of the times. The march of *sepoys* from Meerut to Delhi and declaration of Bahadur Shah Zafar, the last Mughal Emperor as their undisputed leader was the ultimate pointer in that direction.

A Wall of a Heritage Monument, a Dargah in Ahmedabad

Protest as an Instrument of Defiance and Standing Up

Henry David Thoreau remarked, *"Disobedience is the true foundation of liberty. The obedient must be slaves."* Defiance is also a form of protest. Perhaps Adam and Eve were the first humans who defied God and ventured into the forbidden garden with vast consequence for the mankind. Our thriving human civilization would have been inconceivable without their act of disobedience, which was nothing but a mild protest against Almighty's diktat. There must be many mythological characters in all cultural groupings who were great protesters against the ills of their age. In recorded history as well, brave hearts like Socrates, John de Arc and several others took upon themselves to stand for their beliefs and paid by their life. There are instances of Guru ArjanDev during Jahangir's reign and Sarmad during Aurangzeb's period who did not hesitate to make the ultimate sacrifice by defying the royal might.

Protest as an instrument to raise voice against a wrong has thus been with the human race for centuries. Many a protest began with one person and with passage of time gained in strength as more and more people joined to make it a movement or struggle or even an armed rebellion. They may be short-lived or long-drawn, bitter or very violent. In a sense, the home-grown Buddhism, Jainism, Bhakti cult and the Sufi *silsilah* were all protests against the dogmatic beliefs of their era that was arrayed around endless emphasis on outward manifestations of religious practices than its real spirit. The ultimate protest though surfaced in ecclesiastical field in Europe where a group, now probably largest in number as belonging to a religion, actually came to be known in the 16th century as Protestants because they protested against the Roman Catholic Church and its excesses, and are called as such even today.

The French Revolution started with the popular protest about shortage of bread and the Queen Mary Antoinette wondered aloud why they were not eating cake if bread was not available. The American Revolution was about their right to have a say in the taxes. Thus many small beginnings led to developments that totally transformed the political and socio-economic lives of those countries and impacted the world as much. In recent times, the Arab Spring readily comes to our mind, many of these also ending up in violence. But the bloodiest record in recent history is perhaps of Tiananmen Square Massacre (1989) in Beijing, which was scene of massive repression on public protesters.

"There may be times when we are powerless, but there must never be a time when we fail to protest" – remarked Elie Wiesel, how profound! Freedom struggles and movements of nationalities for self-determination have been most burning examples of early protests, gradually transmuting into movements. Our own protest against the colonial rule passed through different phases and finally got consolidated into a unique form and content that left the world gasping in wonder, a largely non-violent struggle that shook the foundation of the mightiest power of the age and forced her to leave. The Civil Disobedience and the Non-cooperation Movements of Mahatma Gandhi were nothing but huge protest against the British policies in India. His non-violent movement occupies a very distinct position in the arena of protest movements the world over. His protest against tyranny was on moral grounds and based on ethical principles. It was the most remarkable statement made by Gandhi in 1942 that *"it is a crime against man and God to submit any more..."* Mahatma's contemporary, Albert Einstein, German physicist who later settled in USA, in another context echoed similar opinion, *"If I were to remain silent, I would be guilty of complicity."*

The protests by students and industrial workers were once very rampant in the country but have since subsided. They often turned ugly leading to loss of life and property, often fanned by political parties who divided these voices amongst themselves and instigated their owners to indulge in activities that went beyond the realm of protest. Some recent protests that caught the imagination of the people were those launched by Anna Hazare, spontaneous protests in Delhi over a horrendous rape case, some related to sit-ins by Aam Aadmi Party etc. These then appeared short-lived but later fructified into substantial development, transforming into an election history.

So perhaps like many other attributes of humans, protest is also unique to them. On a lighter side, animals and plants apparently would not take the protest route, otherwise the beasts of burden would drop their burden every other day, buffaloes would stop giving milk or trees would stop giving us fruits. Luckily it does not happen like that. So humans are happy going around exploiting these poor creatures without appreciating their plight or realizing how quickly we humans react to lodge a protest against the slightest perception of a wrong against our own self. Charity in this case does not begin at home, neither outside. In fact, most of us appear to be immune to the sufferings of animals because the poor animals have no means to protest.

Place Loyalty, Belongingness and Identity

We know about the loyalty bonus points as one of the marketing strategies in the commercial world. So from car companies to airliners to credit card companies, frequent announcements are made to provide mileage points to their users as reward. Brands are also associated with loyalty and prided about. Places, on the same analogy, attract or dispel loyalty worldwide. But, we in India have little to commend on this aspect. Does a *Dilliwala* (Delhiite), a *Hyderabadi* or a Mumbaikar show as strong sense of place loyalty as would be depicted by a Londoner, a New Yorker or a Tokyoite? Unfortunately not! Our cities would be much more livable if that was so. Association with names of individuals and not places is emphasized everywhere by our naming policy. Is this the reason why we lack sense of belongingness to a place?

This is a subject of an objective research. But even without that scholastic support, we may observe a general apathy about that aspect – noticeable even at the national level except by way of right noises due to compelling competitive politics against adversaries. There are larger issues involved and can be debated at great length. However, let us restrict our discussion here to an out of focus area, as one of the possible elements that militates against the development of place loyalty.

The sense of belongingness comes from attachment, good feeling, prestige, social bonding, environment and the totality of positive vibrations about a place. These feelings and emotions in the long run build place identity and loyalty. But we, instead of these, have been fed on personality cult for too long as against a 'place cult', if such a term is acceptable – that too the extent that we begin resembling a North Korean establishment or the erstwhile propagandist State of USSR. Sycophancy, or what a leading newspaper recently carried in its column, *chamchagiri*- series, is the hallmark of our politico-cultural life. The result is that there is hardly any place loyalty per se. What is visible sometimes and mistaken as loyalty is nothing but avoidable acrimonious aggression towards 'others', which then permeates the social life as well.

Historically, our social reforms focused against idol worship. From Bhakti cult to Sufi *sisilah*, the emphasis was on self-effacement, intended to deconstruct individualism and promote social bonding. But these, as also later days saintly preachers like Kabir, Guru Nanak, Swami Vivekanad, Dayanand Saraswati were all made into idols and objects of worship. We thus became concerned with the form rather than the content of their teachings. So the loyalty riveted around the persona as against the philosophy that these great spiritual leaders sought to ensconce. The trend continues and present obsession with this attitude is at an all-time high as 'Babas' proliferate and have tremendous power and clout. This mind-set shuts itself about the significance of a place or even an idea as the other appeal is more emotive and overpowering.

The national leaders are honoured the world over by naming some important institutions or organisations after their names. But we have gone overboard in this matter and show no signs of any rollback. Every institution, university, road, airport, station, bus stand, park, colony has to be named after a personality – worthy or unworthy is not really the question here – it is about the psychology or the mind-set. This unreasonable adulation and sycophancy kills the growth of identification to that institution or place.

Are not our IIMs and IITs great institutions? In fact they are the only ones which really count the world over. They are better off without those name tags with good bonding amongst the alumni, many of whom have contributed to its richness out of loyalty. This is because central to the thoughts of an alumnus is the institution and not a person. If we want to reverse this trend, we need not do much except appending names of these institutions with prefix of some 'worthy' individual and measure the loyalty scale in a few years. The place loyalty would be much less if they were to be named after individuals.

We are so obsessed with this naming business that we invent heroes from the history and thrust them upon the signboards of every possible body. The height of heights is now naming cities after cult figures – there are plenty of them in UP and may be many elsewhere. What kind of place loyalty doe we expect from such names with which most people are not able to relate personally or at an intellectual level.

I was born and raised in a particular town and grew up loving its name and recounting it to myself, my friends and associates and children later. My identity to that place would be disturbed if that name were to be changed. What is being missed is that instead of the place or the organization, the attention is diverted to that perceived or real hero who starts beckoning at us from various circles, junctions or the reception desk of an office, overshadowed by his/her elegantly (un-artistically) framed silhouette. An artistically designed frame of the institution, highlighting the vibrancy of its environmental and cultural ethos would give a larger sense of association and recall value than the picture of a political stalwart about whom one has neither heard nor is there anything to be proud of. Meanwhile one's focus to the institution/place is blurred by this unsolicited visual assault and invasive and surreptitious entry of a character one had not heard of. How would she internalize and talk of an institution/place to her friends or about that framed celebrity who has suddenly appeared in her life like a step-mother to a newly orphaned child and causing dis-orientation. Forgive me; if it sounds trivial, it is not. It would offend any one's sensibilities to be hammered by the names and fames (often fictitious) of these worthies. One would swear by fame of a place or institution and not with a person with whom one has no connect.

India Gate- A Mark of Identity for Delhi

Ideas, Social Change and Resistance

Arthur Schopenhauer said, *"Every truth passes through three stages before it is recognized. In the first, it is ridiculed. In the second, it is opposed. In the third, it is regarded as self-evident"*. Therefore bringing about a social change or a new idea may be considered a very arduous task. It takes shape over many years and may not even happen in the life time of a generation. There is lot of uncertainty involved as well, both in the situation as also for the players. If we look at the great transformation that happened to our freedom movement post-1920, some elements of our discussion will come out clearly. The pettiest constitutional reforms under the British regime, as we know, had just been obtained in the preceding decade, but largely through petitions and resolutions of early nationalists. They deliberated and passed resolutions sitting in committee rooms. They were nationalists no doubt but generally had the belief that the British rule was benevolent and would do some good to the people of the country. They did not challenge its moral foundation. By extension, it also meant that the demand had to be orchestrated through perfectly legitimate methods. We may observe that it was thus a very different perspective and very different way followed by the early leaders of freedom struggle.

This scenario underwent absolute change under Mahatma Gandhi. His civil disobedience movement and *satyagraha* were mass based. He challenged the moral foundation of the British Empire. This approach and strategy totally transformed the freedom struggle. It spilled over from the board rooms to the streets of towns and cities. Another change of another dimension happened around this time in Turkey where their new leader, Kamal Ataturk proclaimed a new constitution modernizing Turkey beyond recognition and promulgating revolutionary ideas like emancipation of women by prohibiting burka and veil and going to the extent of abrogating the institution of *khilafat*(Muslim Caliphate). This would have long lasting impact on the political and cultural contours of the two countries respectively. But we must not forget that efforts of these two statesmen were resisted, opposed, ridiculed and resented in the beginning.

Josiah Gilbert Holland wrote, *"There is no royal road to anything. One thing at a time, all things in succession. That which grows fast, withers as rapidly. That which grows slowly, endures".*So change is slow but dynamic and therefore must be considered positively result-oriented. However, change as we also know, is often ignored initially and sometimes resisted. Change may have different orientations; it could be relating to structure, technology or about processes. It could be about norms, attitudes, habits, like through Information Education Campaign (IEC) or Behavior Change Communication (BCC).

But the most difficult change, which becomes a challenge for its protagonists, is to attempt introducing a new idea. From the earliest times, when the philosophers of new ideas were tortured or put to death, to the French Revolution, Industrial Revolution, Liberalization, et al, ideas passed through several vicissitudes before they came to be accepted. Momentous events in human history leading to clash over ideas, more commonly or largely interpreted as religious or ideological, brought about the most contentious change but unfortunately also led to grave human errors and tragedy. The cult-based philosophy of Nazi Germany and Fascist Italy were responsible for millions of human lives lost. Similarly, the totalitarianism of State and Stalinist purges in the erstwhile Soviet Russia, Cultural Revolution in China and turmoil of political ideas in various countries resulted in large number of killings. Thus the history of ideas is replete with human blood.

Taking the concept of change further ahead, it may be said that it is easily adopted where the society is more loosely structured or its culture is less integrated. Thus, where social dependence is less on each other and where people are more literate and educated and therefore more self-reliant and individualistic, change is more easily accepted. On the other hand, where the society is fully integrated and where communities have lot of mutual dependence, change is more likely to be resisted. It is after all the idea that individual has to change. Only when the individual changes that the collectives of individuals become subject of change. The change of individuals therefore becomes the corner stone of a change management policy, eventually causing the multiplier factor.

While analyzing the difficulties in bringing change or in evaluating the resistance, we may specially underscore some elements. (A) Fear of the unknown: It is generally human to be wary and suspicious of change unless the idea is well conveyed. Thus they fear that the change may be harmful and it may bring about some negativity in their life style or to their families. (B) Distrust: Sometimes the people wanting to introduce change may still be stranger for the change agents or vice versa. Either because of ignorance or because of some negative reputation or mistrust between the two, they become adversaries. (C) Bad timing: Even a good idea can be misconstrued or misunderstood if the time is not ripe for its adoption. (D) Individual stance: It may happen that the individual being approached has little tolerance or has fixed ideas and therefore not susceptible to new ideas. Some of these and many more become or create hurdles in the process of change.

Any change first occurs in the mind of a person and is often in the form of an idea that would gradually take bigger shape and get transported to the field of activity. So it eventually means sharing or rather selling of an idea. This selling of an idea through social marketing is now increasingly relied upon by both private and public players.

THINKING IS NOT ALWAYS OPTIONAL

Hard Work with Smile Women Farmers, in Gujarat Countryside

Women Thy Name is Frailty
Because Men WILL So

Sahir Ludhianvi, the great Urdu poet penned these lines about the plight of Indian women many years ago, *"kitni sadion se ye vahshat ka chalan jari hai/kitni sadion se hai qaym ye gunahon ka rivaj!"*(How long has been this beastly practice in vogue/how long has been this regime of debaucheries against women?). Men have committed most evil atrocities against women and continue to do so. In the land where goddesses are worshipped, women are exposed to many cruelties, forcing them to abort the female fetus being one of these. This and related issues were showcased very effectively in a program produced by Amir Khan and presented on DD National recently as part of the new serial called *'Stya Mev Jayte'*. Typical of Amir, the subject appeared well researched by him on facts and dealt with due diligence, care, sensitivity and intelligence. DG, Doordarshan deserves accolades for this wonderful initiative. Mass awareness must be created for the people to rise against this horrendous primitive practice of killing the girl child.

We must admit that we live in a hypocrite society. We practise retrograde values but in words pay lip service to progressive ideals. Sadly, educated and well off families are equally guilty of the crime of female feticide. The declining sex ratio in most parts of the country, except some matriarchal societies gives a depressing scenario with related social problems. Sex determination is an offence but there is no dearth of clinics and nursing homes in towns and cities that specialise in this 'job'. Our law enforcement and judicial process are as tardy as the public consciousness to be law-abiding. The situation is therefore, grim and calls for extra-ordinary efforts for making a dent. It needs to be examined why is the girl child not valued and how do the perpetrators of this crime get scot free?

The societal value system has been such for generations. There is no qualm about gory discriminatory practices against women. The skin-deep modernity or to use the title of Dipankar Gupta's book, 'mistaken modernity', is what we suffer from. Modernity is limited to wearing western clothes and speaking English in public places. When it comes to showing Western social concerns, most people would wince – the result is stigmatisation of the girl child. The attitude is epitomised in the way women are generally treated in and outside the homes.

The humanist in Sahir propelled him to critique, *"autaar, payambar janti hai/phirbhi Shaitan ki beti hai!"* (Woman begets avatar and prophets/but is still called the devil's daughter). Women are objects of ridicule at the best and lust at the worst. Not surprisingly, cases of crime against women show a rising trend everywhere including domestic violence, molestation, eve teasing, harassment at work and public places etc. Preference for a boy is obsessive that determines the position of women in our society. Earlier most women were not working outside of homes and their monetary input to the household was considered insignificant in the male dominated social order. Notwithstanding the substantive economic contribution of a housewife – a fact that is now increasingly recognised by law courts and given a monetised value that gets added to the savings of a household – with women exceeding in all fields and joining the work force in large numbers, the discriminatory treatment has become all the more unjust and intolerable.

It is largely recognised that reported cases of cruelty to women despite several provisions in law are much lower than the actual instances. Therefore, the social tolerance of such activities is the first stumbling block; most families would try to hide an ugly incident and more so if it happens within the confines of homes at the hands of family members. The false sense of family prestige dictates that outsiders should not know. Then comes a general inhibition on the part of the victim that itself is the result of male-dominated upbringing where women are taught to be submissive and accept minor violations as ways of the world. The poor victim has to be a real brave heart to raise her voice against the perpetrator in the face of combined pressure of the family and the society.

The reporting system and the process of going through the legal rigmarole are heavily tilted against the female victim. All this ensures that either a wronged woman does not get heard or is not able to make a complaint in the first place. Even if she does, the case is so weak and so much deficient in evidence that the possibility of getting any administrative or legal redressal becomes very remote. The system is therefore heavily biased against her. A wronged woman stands a chance only when some feisty woman activist takes up the cudgels on her behalf, or the matter has attracted large-scale media coverage, or if victim is lucky enough to be related to some powerful persons.

There can be no exception to an effective enforcement of existing laws. There are provisions under the PNDT Act that can ensure conviction provided the persecution does an honest and intelligent job. Until the impression is created that there is heavy cost to such misdemeanours, offenders would not be deterred. This needs to be coupled with huge multimedia campaign to build awareness about the position of women in society including rights and entitlements of girls and women through social marketing tools. Women must have the power over their body. Respect for women has to be a learnt social etiquette imbibed through upbringing and early education. It is time we reflect seriously and initiate action. Amir Khan's program is a good beginning in that direction.

Where are the Role Models?

There was a time when children could be given examples of persons as Role Models. That option is closed for several decades. The national leaders who fought for the freedom of our motherland fell in that category without exceptions. There were also those from the fields of art and culture, science, literature, civil service, sports and social service. But, that is past now. The decline has been phenomenal and so sharp that it defies explanation. Is this the price of liberty that we ought to have paid? The ideals of freedom have gone for a toss. The rat race for power and reaches means that no norms are sacrosanct. Liberty has become such a licence in our country today that it is impossible to find a role model for the youth.

It is not fare to categorise a particular class for this downslide as the whole society is responsible for what has apparently gone terribly wrong. The economic progress, though not universal in itself, brought in enormous wealth for certain sections of the society. But along with that came the greed to make instant money and an obsession to succeed at any cost without caring for the means to achieve it. We now have contractors, fixers, brokers and others who liaise and mediate for their protagonists in the corridors of power. Irony is that these persons are not run down, rather they are much sought after; they command a premium amongst the clientele for their specialised jobs. Prosperity has ushered in a consumerist culture that unabashedly professes acquisitions, richness, power and influence, not necessarily in that order and at the cost of morality, equity, fairness and democratic principles. The emergence of this vile institution of brokerage typically means that there is no level-playing field for ordinary hard-working persons as success would ordinarily come from extraneous factors. Unfortunately this is no longer an isolated situation and too wide-spread to ignore, and worse, is almost becoming a mass psyche for the attainment of worldly riches. Ethical practices have become a huge casualty in that process — they are now out of fashion and aren't even spoken of. So, we are reconciled to live a life like this even as a society with wants falls easy prey to crutches and promissory notes that are expected to deliver.

It is not the case that the change is to be resisted as that would be against the law of nature. The trend is unstoppable. With higher standards of life, neither the unrelenting demand for more goods (luxuries) and services will cease nor the insatiate urge to buy and acquire more and more. But what must be inculcated gradually is the attitude to acquire only through legitimate means. High disposable income sources are often suspect and are expended on activities that are not honourable. The problem is, ethics cannot be taught to adults. It is something that comes from environment in which one grew — inherited and imbibed from the family and the immediate social circles — a toll order to ensure such exposure and training to the general population. But initiative must be made in that direction and the best way is to 'catch them young'. Some internal control mechanism and self-imposed discipline may be inculcated in the youth to begin with.

The question then comes where to begin and from who? We may recall the famous adage, *Jaisa Raja, WaiseeParja*'(you get the government that you deserve). Therefore, the change of mindless splurge as against mindful spending should come from the political class as they are rich, have the propensity to spend more and are in command; this may be followed by similar obligation from other influential classes from the Corporates, Bureaucracy, Business, rich farmers and others. The ostentatious spending, made possible by large money that these classes hold, is infectious for the less endowed who without the wherewithal, try to replicate the practices of the 'upper classes" and therefore fall prey to debts, bankruptcy or worse, resort to getting the money from illegitimate sources. A word of caution — illegitimate earning is more the preserve of the powerful, many of whom succeeded through dubious means — it is never the case that the deprived would have the proclivity to adopt such means. But, they are likely to be influenced to do the same through the working of the theory of demonstration effect.

Our Constitution provides certain code of conduct but is regrettably disregarded. We may specially refer to the Preamble, the Directive Principles and the Fundamental Duties. If followed and implemented effectively, they may provide the moral-legal framework for promoting ethical practices in public life.

Importantly, Moral Science and some basic knowledge of Indian laws must be reintroduced to our youngsters. While the former has remained tucked-in as a neglected portion of the school curricula with uninspiring presentation and insipid content, which is barely equipped to impart the youth a value-based education with necessary ethical learning, the lack of knowledge about the latter has kept them unaware about the basic civil and criminal laws of the land that could act as a deterrent against wrong. Some of this age group may then be expected to grow up as role models for their next generation.

Medical Care and the Family Physician

The health delivery system in our country is largely dependent on government hospitals for treatment and hospitalisation. Private treatment is expensive and mostly out of reach for the poor. Medical care is also increasingly getting highly specialised as the return for specialists as also for the private hospitals that employ them is far more rewarding. There is no case against specialities; they serve a very useful purpose by providing better diagnosis and treatment. But in a deficit scenario it militates against the general good as fewer and fewer get specialised investigations and treatment while large numbers are denied basic medical attention. It is in this context that one may think of the need of a general physician (GP) who until some years back treated the whole family and was the most reliable doctor next door. The talk here centers on an urban landscape as needs of rural health care, itself a huge issue, would need a more elaborate discussion; though a GP is as indispensable in a village scenario where life is more community-oriented.

The family doctor was a great institution in the good old days and he was mostly a GP. Many of us would have the vivid memory of that visiting doctor – almost an extinct species now – to our homes whose brief case as children we carried to his car after he had seen almost every member of the family. Going to his modest clinic was equally easy as he was in the neighbourhood and was easily accessible. The fee that he took for his service was pea nuts. More than that, he showed deep care and empathy not only for the patients but also very good understanding of the ailment(s) that he was treating. He was part of the community and could treat as well as tender advice to families on matters of preventive health. The institution as a bulwark of basic community medical care has declined of late, leaving a gap and increasing the cost of health care.

The reasons for this may be debated. But some apparent developments may be noted here.As life started getting complicated and consumerism increased the demand for more specialised medical care increased manifold. The quality of health care is now more assessed in terms of opulence of the place, décor – an appropriate ambience and add-ons. Upgradation of services is a positive thing and has actually been a pressing need as government hospitals often wear shabby looks and largely show no regard for making the place cleaner and tidy. That objective has been met to a good extent by expansion of medical services at the hands of private sector. The private hospitals are cleaner, better organised and appear more cheerful. That culture, if not the atmosphere, is very slowly but definitely filtering down to some extent in government hospitals at least in better governed states. Hence standardisation of services by private sector as also the generally improved ambience of the hospitals has been a positive development.

But a fall out of this newer development has been the increasing inaccessibility and rising cost of such places, which have become prohibitive and beyond the reach of the vast majority of the people. Even modest clinics and nursing homes are found to be charging hefty fees and therefore unaffordable even for the middle classes, what to talk of the urban poor. This demand generated by big players in the medical profession has meant more pressure for specialities in medical colleges and the simultaneous decline in the prestige of the good old 'simple MBBS'. Shorn of glamour and less in demand, the basic medical degree and its practitioner have both lost grounds to their competitors. This has led to disappearance of the family physician who was so much visible in the by lanes of our towns and who performed a very useful community service in an inexpensive way. We need to revive the glory of 'simple MBBS' who practised as GP.

The GP is good at symptomatic treatment without always going for diagnostic investigations in all cases. He helps in cutting the cost of treatment, in avoiding the cost of hospitalisation and providing instant medical care with greater convenience. He is also more dependable being available in the vicinity and without the rigmarole of registration, advance booking etc. The social needof health care to the maximum number was met through this institution in a big way and in an unobtrusive manner.

With changing times newer demands are put on the system – medical specialities and more organised medical care have to be seen in that context, and that is but natural. What is, however, unnatural is the aided and abetted casting of a shadow on the family doctor and his related eclipse. Our society still badly needs this community based healer who comes at lower cost as a parallel mechanism for greater good. But perhaps he also needs to be repackaged. We have the disciplines of community medicine, preventive medicine, wellness etc. A more compact course, say just about six months could be devised for aspirants willing to practise as family doctors (MBBS) with some incentives by the state. This specially devised short course would equip our GPs with advanced knowledge concerning family health issues and newer techniques to address ailments. It is expected that this focused approach would help in creating demand for this declining institution and in reviving this segment of medical profession for strengthening the gap in community medical care.

The Act of Giving and Us

The recent annual survey report of the World Giving Index (WGI) about Indians has gladdened our heart. It was informed that as compared to people of many other nationalities, Indians ranked higher this year for volunteering their time and donating money. This marker was found distinct in contrast to the Chinese for example. We have no idea what Chinese do of their time and money. But talking of our own selves, this assumption of WGI seems to be based on a misreading of what is going on. Most of us must not have seen any good number of people volunteering time and money for others, or for a cause. Can we readily think of individuals, neighbours, even friends and relatives who are doing this on regular basis? We have not observed any such noticeable trend across the people and cities known to us. There are only exceptions, if any, both in terms of names and the regularity of participation by such individuals. The report therefore may have to be taken with a pinch of salt. We may also analyze its basis and what could have prompted such an assessment.

It is not the case that we are insensitive to the needs of others or to the act of giving. All of us have our ways of doing charity. But typically in our country, it's mostly community-driven. There are indeed groups and organizations who are involved in distributing food, clothes etc to the poor in special locations. There are others who set up camps to extend relief to the victims of floods and other natural disasters. These efforts are supported by well-meaning individuals who want to help others. But often these efforts are for currying favour with the gods. Our trigger is the desire to secure good position in the world hereinafter. Giving alms to the poor is an act of piety that will bring the blessings of gods or goddesses. So when we give, we do a *punya* (Hindu), a *sawaab*(Muslim) and thereby earn Almighty's goodwill. Without undermining the value and utility of such aids that provide succor to the needy, it is clear that most of our giving is driven by the diktat of religion and guided by the expectation of reward - an eternal life of peace and happiness – guaranteed by the alms giving. At a personal level the philosophical context of our giving is mainly religious.

Albert Schweitzer said, *"Wherever you turn, you can find someone who needs you. Even if it is a little thing, do something for which there is no pay but the privilege of doing it. Remember, you don't live in a world all of your own"*. We have reputed NGOs managed by dedicated men and women who volunteer their time for a cause, among them, we may recall HelpAge India, Goonj, Pratham, Udaan, Smile Foundation etc. just to name a few and there are many more. But the same cannot be said about tens of thousands NGOs who keep springing up now and then everywhere. Therefore, while many are doing great work and deserve our respect, involved here again, are several individuals whose best contribution is by way of some monthly financial contribution, rather than an active physical participation to reach the communities being attended to. And often the call taken is more for social recognition than driven from any serious commitment to the cause itself. There is no objection to recognition or even publicity of a work and of persons involved with such activities as it encourages the participants and acts as a morale booster. But sometimes that desire becomes the primary motivation behind such exertions, than an intellectual conviction to volunteer time and money. In that situation the long term sustainability of such acts may be suspect as removal of the lime light becomes a dampener, i.e. because they are not getting recognition and publicity they will sulk and stop contributing.

As for the religious fervor for the act of giving it is community-oriented and generally restrictive and exclusive in practice. The conceptual framework of such activities is derived from scriptures and therefore linked to the theory of reward and punishment and not from a sense of social responsibility per se, which would make these more inclusive and broad based.

We may therefore start looking at this scenario from another perspective; or rather trace the lack of a perspective, namely, 'secular giving', if such a phrase could be used. However, since secularism itself has fallen into disrepute and become a derogatory term these days, it may have to be cautiously explained and determined. It is only meant here to signify that this giving is not ordained by religious beliefs, ordinarily linked to attainment of *jannat* or *swarg* (heaven) but steered by a mere social sense of responsibility felt for others who are less endowed. Such motive, broadly termed as humanism is intellectually supported by recognition to fulfill a reciprocal societal role and is guided by ethical principles. The inspired person is dictated to give or extend help not because the scriptures say so but because of his inner voice, his humanism, his sense of reasoning, in short without theism. The guidance here comes from consciousness and the soul; it is driven by conscience, almost a sense of personal obligation. So it is not imposed from an external belief system but guided from an internal control mechanism.

It was observed by Richelle E. Goodrich, *"It's impossible to be involved in all situations, but there is no excuse not to be involved in something, somewhere, somehow, with someone. Make an ounce of difference"*. Our commitment and contribution in that sense is too less evident to be put at such a high pedestal as erroneously done by the World Giving Index.

Religions and Religiosity

Man's search for meaning of life took him to gods and gradually to spirituality. Religion evolved to answer his fears, insecurities, matters of life and death, complexity of troubled times, solace in grief and to satisfy the urges for reaching the sublime. Interestingly the search for gods appeared in one or the other form in all social formations; so from Atlantic to Pacific to the Mediterranean to the Indian Ocean, the quest sprang from the earliest era of human civilisation - from primordial to myths and rituals to tribal to cultural and finally in its present organised form. These were carried forward as much through the scriptures as by the oral traditions.

Gradually, the pursuit of search for the truth and mysteries of life moved from personal to cosmic. Religion got systematically organised and now has all the trappings of power, pomp and glory. It is considered as one of the most flourishing professions riding over immeasurable fixed assets and turnovers running into hundreds of thousands of crores. However, religion serves some social purposes as well - teaches the followers good moral conduct, piety, charity, kindness, peace, honesty and goodness. Further, it helps out in controlling the baser instincts of humans - selfishness, arrogance, jealousy, ill-will, crookedness etc. It inculcates the feeling of brotherhood among its own community and counsel tolerance for others - some persons follow a different path, is another story. Finally, it promotes spirituality – by surrendering one's ego and subjugating one's desires, nay one's mind and soul before an unknown power, humans aspire to attain heavenly blessings for a life of peace and piety and a divine life hereafter.

In the Indian context, from Budhism to Ashoka's Dhamma to Guru Nanak's teachings to the *Bhakti* expositions to the *Sufi silsila* - all being catholic in views, eclectic in approach and opposed to bigotry - a strand of moralistic life devoid of selfishness and full of sacrifice, piety and total surrender to the Supreme Being was emphasised. All of them discouraged the adherents from spreading mischief and strife and exhorted them to attain righteousness for achieving higher order of life. The Belief system was not only a cementing force; it was a source of strength for the devotees. Abroad, the earliest Judeo-Christian traditions, the later Christian wisdom and the Islamic teachings advanced the same moralistic life in one form or the other for one and all.

Unfortunately, this idealism has been lesser in practice and more in its breach. Worst excesses have been committed in the name of religion against the "other" by adherents of each religious group through the ages, as also against one's own for blasphemy and heretical declarations. There were also curbs on personal freedom, and life's choices. Often it became regressive - some of these traits have continued and visible even today. Some believe that many retrograde social customs and restrictions are sanctioned by religions and therefore how good are the diktats of faith?

It is in this background that we need to look at the increasing religiosity in our country, as distinct from a spiritual yearning or a basic belief in a cosmic world order. Religiosity is more to do with the form and outer manifestations of a preferred religion and the dogmatic outlook of its practitioners. Clearly, religiosity has not been able to create righteousness in human beings, in promoting inter and intra-religion dialogues, and in establishing a tolerant and syncretic belief-system. It has not promoted honesty, sensitivity to the feelings and need of others, good neighbourliness, care and concern; it has neither curbed bigotry, viciousness, selfishness, egotism, greed and dishonesty of its adherents. Religiosity has not been able to reduce from the society mischief, corruption, prejudice, hostility, animosity, violence and criminality. It is commonplace to find many persons of deviant behaviour outwardly religious and punctilious to the religious rituals. Paradoxically, more religiosity sometimes means more self-centredness and intolerance. Would the God(s) be appeased by performance of *yatras*, *haj* and pilgrimages, especially when so much wrong happens in the name of religion? Perhaps these individuals or groups are faking to be religious or there is something wrong with religiosity itself.

Sadly we talk less of humanism and scientific temper, which runs as a parallel stream of thought but is in a state of rejection in the 21st century - incidentally rationalism was more current in the 19th and 20th centuries than it is today. Starting with Enlightenment, it inspired many generations, gave birth to new ideas and propelled many scientific discoveries, cultural effervescence, flourishing of fine arts, setting up of seats of higher learning, philanthropic works etc. And more than that, it promoted objectivity in the study of humanity, subjects like history, literature and sociology, encouraged rational inquiry and development of a scientific outlook that was less constrained by subjectivity. It was fashionable in the 70s and 80s to show irreverence to religiosity; it is chic now to flaunt your religiosity.

That brings us to the last part of the discussion - 'religion vs spirituality and inner consciousness'. It is not to suggest that they are mutually contradictory because they are not. On the other hand, they are inseparable and mutually complimentary. It is the divorce between the two that creates the chasm and discord. In the best traditions of every religion, spiritualism should inform our religious belief-system or religiosity. A truly spiritual person cannot be anything but good and nothing can be more spiritual than spreading love and goodness.

We may conclude by quoting poet philosopher, Dr. Muhammad Iqbal from his *'Naya Shiwala'*, *"shakti bhi shaanti bhi bhakton ke geet me hai/dharti ke baasiyon ki mukti preet me hai"*(both power and peace emanate from the songs of devotees/salvation for the dwellers of this earth lies in love).

A Temple, Goa

A Mosque, Goa

Living Apart - the Cultural Divide

We in this country are faced with economic disparities that perpetuate a huge divide in the society. That divide is galling and an embarrassment for a modern democratic mind. Unfortunately, the reality cannot be wished away. But there is another dimension to the chink in our society, that is, a deep cultural crevice. This traverses across regions, communities, and metros. It appears as if we live simultaneously in different centuries and in different worlds - time and space suddenly appear into spatial relief. The manifestations of this split are witnessed in ghettoisation of communities, the contrast no better than, between a gated community and a pocket of slum in any of our metros. On the face of it, this difference has to do with economic status of these two segments. There is no denying that economics is a determinant of the cultural mores of a given community or society. But beyond what meets the eyes are the socio-cultural practices, followed in independent human silos. The context would be understood by watching a well-off modern lady who saunters in a fashionable street and runs into a sari clad Rajasthani woman selling pillow covers. Culturally they are alien to each other, they speak different languages, dress differently; their food habits, their world view have nothing to compare.

On a different plane, think of our modes of transports from Ferrari to the animal cart, from Rajdhani and Shatabdi trains to the drag machines that connect the mofussil towns across the length and breadth of India, from

BMW taxi to the *FutFutsewa* of Old Delhi - all hang together. In fact, very few countries can boast of such ancient varieties of vehicles jostling for space with the best from the stable of auto giants. We have the luxury-liners with five star facilities on board, compared to ramshackle contraptions that pass as ships and sail in inland waters and routinely capsize.

We have the IIMs, IITs, highly acclaimed medical and scientific institutions, research centers, fast growing private universities and colleges. There are swanky schools, air-conditioned class rooms in Wi-Fi campuses with high-end sporting facilities and state of the art auditoriums. And we also have schools with non-existent rooms with no desks or blackboards. But the cake is taken by the *'charwahavideyalaya'* - where the pupil is actually taking his lesson sitting atop the buffalo.

Our health facility offers another sharp contrast. There are hospitals that now cater to even American and European clientele - medical tourism is catching up in India - who finds world class facilities in these modern institutions at relatively lower costs. And we have people being treated and actually undergoing surgeries in open camps. There are toilets fitted with Jacuzzi and Spa in many homes and we have half the population of the country without access to basic toilet facility for protecting their dignity.

All these create insurmountable cultural and psychological barriers. They sustain biased stereotypes about each other. Lack of communication reinforces the prejudices and accentuates differences. We may, therefore, come to the next stage of identifying the dynamics of this situation. Why is this divide, especially the psychological segregation so pronounced and so much visible? There are two reasons for this - the lack of equitable education and the absence of a common lingua franca in the country.

The fault line of our educational system is too apparent to be described at length. First, the erroneous nomenclature - an oxymoron - namely the so-called public schools! We call the private schools as public, which is a joke; the real public schools are the government schools with all their inadequacies. We have neglected the government schools so thoroughly that every person with the slightest means of affordability tries to put his child in a 'public school'. Our educational system is a huge de-equaliser that promotes and perpetuates cultural distinction between people. In general also there is a huge disparity in quality of education from urban to semi-urban and rural areas. Those who go through less endowed institutions constitute the 'cultural have-nots'.

Our education system provides the defining moment of social and cultural divisiveness.

As regards our 'link language', that is still under wraps - all hell will let loose if one were to talk of Hindi as the national language. It is another matter that it is one language that is understood and spoken in all parts of the country. But unfortunately, it suffers from huge inhibition. It is not proudly owned by well-educated people even from the so-called Hindi heartland. Other regional languages have the same fate. The knowledge of spoken English is the symbol of having been brought up well. Howsoever proficient a person may be in his own subject, arts, science, music or sports, he cannot command respect with an audience unless he is adept in English. Hockey, football and volleyball are lagging behind because their players are mostly speakers of the regional languages but golf, cricket, badminton and tennis prosper as their patrons are English speaking. So sports where we excelled have fallen through for cultural reasons while English heritage of the adopted games gives them a boost. Language or more precisely, the absence of a pan-Indian link language keeps alive cultural distinction between groups of people. In this scenario, the twin task of universalizing quality education and restoring faith and pride in our Indian languages may help in bridging the cultural divide among the populace.

How Equal Are We?

The expression 'son in law mentality' was found to have been used somewhere during 1980s in a write-up by Swami Ranganathananda who was an enlightened social thinker. The allusion in his comment was to the strong desire of every person to be given special treatment as distinct from what is being accorded to all others. The hallmark of that mentality as we understand is a system based on privileges. This should not surprise anybody. The wish to be treated differently and deferentially is very strong in all humans but singularly overpowering amongst us Indians. It is almost a national obsession. The political class may appear to lead this race but each one of us is equally conscious to be given particular attention. To want to be distinct is not an undesirable thing. But distinction at the cost of the fellow travellers and based on lineage or birth alone may not be as honourable. But that is what we crave for. This is neither democratic nor a modern attitude.

We have come across interesting situations during public functions and ceremonies when certain persons are noticed making desperate attempts to seek the center-stage of attention by hook or crook; it is both hilarious and pathetic. They would try very hard to be noticed and then prevail upon the organisers to accord them some degree of deference, and thereby make them look different from the crowd. The mixed look of somberness and triumph on their faces, once that objective is attained, is something to marvel about but it also gives them away. You can almost read their mind. The adulation-seekers are expert in making others look obsequious and in enforcing obeisance. It gives great pride to the practitioners of this art in claiming and enforcing reverence for themselves.

How has this become a way of life with us? As we try to decode the genetic composition of this class of people, some meaning starts emerging. It is rightly said that man is the product of the environment in which he grows. Perhaps the reason lies in a general non-recognition of meritocracy in our society. Even merit, incidentally is often recognised only after it is first propped up by some powerful groups/individuals/agencies or through help coming from some extraneous circumstances. No wonder, we have always rejoiced in ancestry, whether blue blood or acquired; status consciousness is overriding. This status is based on birth or on the basis of what our parents or in-laws did or earned earlier, or on privileges acquired through dubious means.

There seems to be lack of internalisation of a democratic ethos. Dominant thinking still thrives at spoil system.Though we had proto-democratic institutions in the earliest phases of our history, the institutions got gradually decimated even as feudalism under the patronage of royalty sprang its tentacles and took deeper roots in our society. And feudalism was not just an economic system as many may think. It was a retrograde socio-psycho-cultural construct, based on privileges that flourished on deeply held differentiation between the haves and the have-nots – it was actually a relationship of servitude – where the latter looked at the former as the *'annadata'/'maibaap'*. The institution of feudalism has apparently waned but more in its physical manifestation. Its stronghold over the minds remains. Many of us still have not come out of that serfdom syndrome. The result is that some people are able to manipulate the system to project and establish their superiority over others, and the latter acquiesce into it. The stratification in the society is a function of the feudal mind-set.Feudal behaviour in a democratic polity, an oxymoron in terms, is nevertheless a hard fact of the Indian life even into the 21st century. Democracy does not recognise feudalism. Healthy democratic idea would not covet privileges. So it is clear that egalitarian awareness has not taken roots in our society. Merit-based claim to position and status is still a far cry.

Yet another aspect may be looked at. Is this mind-set the product of centuries of caste system that prevailed in the country? The deleterious effects of caste system on our society and polity is another subject altogether and not in focus here. However, to make the short point, this social stratification has actively aided and abetted the formation of a privilege based social structure. In fact, caste system and feudalism are mutually complimentary and help in sustaining each other. Together they promote the privilege based order. All this get reflected in the attitude of the advantaged sections. It would not be easy to break this twin shackle of feudal outlook and caste system. Sustained quality education may be used to awaken humanism, egalitarianism and democratic convictions to emancipate us from this socio-cultural malaise.

Bringing Up and Other Issues

By the time children pass the high school they are at the threshold of adulthood and career – facing portents of a volatile phase of psychological and emotional upheavals. The uncertainties of life ahead, peer and family pressure for securing high grades, expectations of parents, the prospect of leaving their best friends and other emotional and relationship issues put tremendous pressure upon them to perform, to show good conduct and all that. Torn between conflicting demands and their own inner turmoil, accentuated by a desire to be independent of outside controls, they tend to reflect hidden anxiety and the resultant irritation in their attitudes.

The system of education and the kind of pressure that is built around the course structure is not helpful either. The priority is not learning and acquisition of life skills but a blind race to achieve, to march past others and steal the show at whatever cost. At a juncture when youngsters feel threatened by the prospect of losing a community with which they identified and felt comfortable with, and nervous about missing togetherness of the known world, the pressure to excel adversely impacts their sense of well-being and impairs the feeling of belongingness - alienation from the world around is therefore not uncommon - the unbearable pressure creates Zombies of some young men and women.

We have the digital world now that offers the young folks an escape route and an opportunity to get into an impersonal, make-believe voyeuristic world that acts as vend to their tired mind and soul. They get connected to a nameless outside world but become oblivious to their own immediate surroundings. Thus a surreal world is woven around that is somehow more soothing and acceptable to their frayed nerves.

For a psychologically healthy and emotionally sound personality, these are not the best situations. What perhaps is lacking is the absence of an institutional culture in the schools that should provide support and sustenance and help them to absorb the vagaries of change and pressure faced by their psychic being. It has been said, "to grow old is natural, to grow up responsibly is optional". Is the system helping them in growing up responsibly, is the question we need to ask.

Talking of institutional culture, it plays a crucial role in developing special traits in alumnus of a particular institution, which last a life-time. A good institution gives some tangibles like quality education, a branded degree and extra-curricular achievements. There are also intangibles, which cannot be measured but hold a lot of value including an inherent confidence, sense of belonging and long-term camaraderie with a group. The enduring association and net-work so created gives psychological advantage that goes to build the overall persona of such individuals. A healthy and positive institutional culture facilitates the development of a grounded and rounded personality.

But in the race to "succeed" in life, the emphasis in class-room teaching is entirely focused on Science and Technology, Medicine and Engineering, Computer Sciences and Informatics Practices, Commerce and Economics. These subjects are expected to ensure a student's marketability as he climbs the career ladder. In the process, a very old subject known as Civics has been relegated to a backseat. It is not part of the core subjects, shorn of glamour; it is not even offered if option is available. Moreover, the content of the subject has stagnated – it has not been suitably revised so as to keep pace with the changing needs and mores of the society. This neglect is proving costly to the country as may be seen from the general behaviour of even adults who do not observe widely acceptable social norms, let alone following the laws of the land.

There are many concerns that can be highlighted and brought centre-stage through serious study of this subject, so that youngsters develop more responsible social manners. How do we curb an 'elbow society' – a construct where each one of us tries to push past the other, whether it is while driving in the street or while trying to snatch somebody else's opportunity, position, work, name, brand, copyright and so on. The next question is what type of city we want to live in or a country to be proud of. A place is made beautiful not only by its monuments and buildings but made so by its inhabitants, by their attitude to others, by their civility, care and concern, by their good behaviour. Unless a contribution is made by each person to develop ownership of public spaces and issues, change will not happen. It is important to bequeath a better world to the next generation than the one that was inherited. This inter-generational equity is crying for attention in every field of our life.

Some ethical questions that may be put to youngsters in the citizenship education program may be like this:

a) Where would you like to see yourself 10-15 years from now?
b) What would you like to be known for?
c) What is it that would give you pride when you look back?

If we are able to revive Civics, especially citizenship education program as a core curriculum in schools for training young minds, the downside of cut-throat competition will be mitigated to some extent, avoiding co-lateral damages and in making better citizens out of our young men and women. They would then be better equipped to steer and navigate the country by the time they take up the leadership.

ANGULAR VISION
OF THINGS

Émigrés are the Chosen Ones!

Humans are considered rational beings who dare to think. Thinking may sometimes go haywire, is another matter. It's this human trait that pushed me into trying to unravel an official, or should I say an officious development. A massive transfer list of IAS officers had been issued. It was declared to be 'routine transfers'. That left the ball rolling. Pressing my brain I thought of drawing parallels or looking for analogies for decoding the issue at hand.

Let us recall the history of cheap indented labour in Asia and Africa during the 18th and 19th centuries, which were relocated in large numbers by the European colonialists to East and West Indies. We may also recall the plight of convicted persons deported to penal settlements in far flung areas. The poor guys were driven line sink and hooker to totally new settings far away from homes. They suddenly found themselves in totally unfamiliar environs and amidst an alien culture. On arrival they found that they could not even converse with the local populace; their food habits were different, dressing was unaccustomed. None of the familiar indicators were available to which they could relate. The settlers of course did not know then that a time might come when some of them would be high and mighty of those settlements.

Moral of the story: these unwise guys moaned and grieved because they could not comprehend their position. They lacked philosophical insight to look at the distant future, which beckoned a beam of light. Had these persons been gifted with a vision they could have foreseen their bright future and would not have complained so bitterly to their benefactors (read handlers) on being deployed to far flung territories for their 'purported' upliftment.

Life has reached a full circle as a bunch of bureaucrats under transfer to far off territories in comparable situation are grimacing, showing lot of anxiety and nervousness. They have become grouchy and started grumbling and sulking; their naiveté is deplorable. They would deserve no sympathy but as a concession to their families, they need not be condemned for their immature behaviour. It is because of their ignorance that they are being ungrateful to their guardian angels (read competent authority); it's nothing but sheer ludicrousness on their part. Forgive them Lord for they know not what they are doing!

These transferees have failed to appreciate that just as religious philosophies demand compliance with observance of certain practices and rituals for the attainment of rewards for life hereinafter, government system demands adherence to certain infallible diktat for future laurels. There is no justification in raising hue and cry over transfers that were issued in the best interests of these uninformed incumbents. They are missing out the sublime truth and the transcendental schemes of the cosmic order. Is the benevolent system to be blamed or the uninformed bureaucrats who have no superior instincts to comprehend the inspiring philosophy? Like the indented ancestors of earlier era they are shouting hoarse looking at the darker side of the picture. Regrettably they fail to visualise umpteen possibilities that such transfers (read dislocations) offer.

Optimism should never be allowed to wane, much less in times of upheavals, simply because one is barely able to see the future and its numerous possibilities. Some might find their soul-mates at new places while others a spare, or a better replacement of the existing burden. Some others would be able to build new hearth and business in the novel surroundings. The insulated lifestyle at some of these territories is pregnant, literally with promises that would be inconceivable at the old abode with peeping toms and envious neighbours.

So when the call comes in the life of a bureaucrat to 'migrate', even if involuntarily, he must know that there is not to reason why but to do or die. He should at once break himself away from the mesh of *moh, maya* (materialistic trappings) and not be unnerved by such mundane orders. Instead he should rejoice and consider himself to be the chosen one who has been entrusted with and is being entreated for the attainment of certain higher objectives. He should not forget that a tornado that uproots many trees also promotes the redevelopment of the devastated place into a salubrious, sylvan surrounding. In case the transfer entails family or filial break-up or worse, so be it. The solace to the brave hearts must come from a spiritual mind that considers such collateral damages as trivial in a world that is nothing but *mayaa-jaal or mrigtrishna*(magical spell or mirage). One needs to open up the inner eyes. God help those who are not the owner of a mystical frame of mind. So happy landing folks!

Why Could Not I Read
the Newspaper!

Life's uncertainties and unpredictability are both mirthful and mysterious. Not trivializing but exploring my own circumstances, I discovered that I am often not able to read the morning newspaper, something that holds infinite attraction for me otherwise. Some serious effort at recollecting the sequence of events in the morning led to the eventual unearthing of what kept the distance between me and the daily happening around the world. It must not be lost sight of that there has never been a monotony in the position of each day. In fact every morning brings its own set of circumstances, though frankly I sometime vaguely suspect but can never imagine indulging in such insinuations that they may be a well-planned and dexterously executed ploy or examples of brilliant craftsmanship calculated to keep me away from those lovely pages. Some amazing event just leaps out every morning from nowhere and the newspaper remains as hard to pin down as a slippery fish. A round-up of events on a certain morning may help the readers in appreciating what usually transpires.

The morning in question began with a very harmless and earnest-sounding, pleasant as hell request from my better half for a cup of tea, which as a good husband I could never find fault with. Having finished that first chore of a dutiful, perpetually obliged looking husband, I sauntered along to my den with the empty tray in my hands, wearing a new-found confidence on my face for having completed the task – just the way our Tommy looks immediately after picking up the rubber bone on being commandeered to do so – with that precious piece of paper tugged under my unwashed morning underarms. My reverie for immediately delving into my dream world of to-be-acquired-knowledge was broken as I was very politely and sweetly called out not to forget 'just plugging in' the washer-dryer, which I was communicated has already been readied with clothes and detergent. I was impressed no end, as I always am several times every day with her level of competency and 'workwomanship'. I already found myself savouring the intimacy of my ultimate joy, the morning newspaper.

While I was entangled in trying to figure out which point actually triggers the contraption to life and gives me a sense of achievement – I must confess being quite a technology-immune kind of a guy – I heard another sugary and endearingly winning tone imploring me for making a phone call to a particular person who apparently specializes in designing clothes, an euphuism for our good-old neighbourhood lady's tailor and whose non-arrival in next two hours could lead to a major catastrophe. As I strut past after finishing these activities and still managed to look cheerful for having done my bit to the morning household chore, there was an ominous shriek. I fumbled and collided with the chairs while sprinting to liberate that owner of the shrill squeal from any calamitous grip. It transpired that a tiny lizard has just been discovered and life would not be the same again until that little monster is driven out from the site of those dignified but frightened hazel eyes, which were though very tightly closed by then and which no amount of cajoling would ever be able to open up.

The game of hide and seek began between this divine-seeker of truth and the minuscule, sneaky creature, in the vain hope of attaining the larger objective, namely, a glimpse of the morning newspaper. While the commander of my house and my life too, kept sitting in a corner, tight fisted, jaws clenched with her eyes still shut, mostly oblivious to the fracas except some occasional screams then and now; all this while her demeanor so downcast as if she would not live another day. It could melt the heart of the unkindest person on the earth. For this pursuer of truth, finding and driving out that swine from the confines of our house became the ultimate challenge and it took more than an hour to do so.

The fracas had meanwhile taken its toll and my ultimate standard of beauty was in need of caring affection and some spirit boosting talk. I told her not to worry, that the imp was driven out. Then suddenly in an indiscreet moment, I blurted out that her anxiety neurosis was uncalled for; I became conscious of my damaging last statement even before it came out of my mouth. As a damage-control exercise, I immediately started off on a long list of wife-enticing phrases. One of this to my memory was, "Honey, I love you the way you are". This one from me and the fact that she had luckily missed my last statement, perhaps due to her stupor, saved my day.

When such dreadful occurrence happens, her electrolytes drop down and so a glass of fresh lime water is a must and a mood elevator. So, that was arranged double quick by the smitten husband. Meanwhile since the morning tea had become a casualty owing to the commotion, and reheated tea is not preferred, I was most faithfully obligated to go around the burner once again.

Since we aren't exactly match and gasoline, I get down to this 'ungruelling' schedule without any murmur like a faithful husband that I am. Though my usual doubts about the theories of existence etc. resurface and life goes on.

Couch Potato does No Justice to Potato!

Solanumtuberosum, potato in plain English is said to have been originally cultivated in the region of Peru from where it gradually moved during the 16th century onward to Europe and America and later to the rest of the world. Today, China, India, Russia, Ukraine, America and Germany are the major producers of this food crop, followed by others. It is estimated that three-fourths of the world population depends on this item for their daily food needs. It has many essential nutrients required to fill the physical energy needs of humans, like carbohydrates, fat, protein, vitamins and trace metals. We could not have asked for more.

Many vegetables and fruits that we take today as a given, were just not there for our ancestors, a couple of centuries earlier. Potato is one such versatile item of food on our table today which was not known to the mighty kings, Ashoka, Kanishka and even Akbar. What a pity they missed out on *alooparantha, aloodum, alookofte, aloopaalak* and several other such delectable Indian dishes! But at least those kings and their queens were spared being called names then like 'couch potato' as is the common wont today for the comfort-seeking guys like us. This is nothing but sacrilege to malign such a nice 'vegetable- partner' – it so effortlessly goes along with several other vegetables. Something that is so conveniently accessible and useful cannot be given a derogatory acronym. If anything, it is so portable and is literally going places. It is not fair at all to call potato *mota* and so on.

As young children, we read that Potato was the staple food in countries like Ireland and Belgium. But to me, it is today the staple food in India as well. In fact, it may perhaps be the third staple diet after rice and wheat in most parts of the world, India included. Which family would miss this item as part of at least one meal a day, around the length and breadth of the country and the year round? Even the Biryani in Kolkata, sometimes Awadhi *Biryani* and *Qalia*, a scrumptious dish of mutton, cooked over slow flame for an extended time also has potato in it – big chunks of light fried potato, generally big in size cut into two pieces. Kolkata *dum biryani* (slowly cooked in sealed steam of its own) is a wonderful dish and the potato pieces soaked in the juice of Biryani and Qalia taste delicious. Potato is of course the vegetarians' delight. *Dosa, tikkichaat, samosa* and *pau-bhaji* are inconceivable without the use of potato as a major ingredient in these Indian delicacies. Our present generation would die if they were denied burger and French fries, coming from this *mota* fellow.

India is perhaps the second largest producer of potato in the world after China. It is one staple diet that we eat in all seasons and all times of the day. Think of the chips and its other variants that are available in every nook and corner of the country, even in the remote village. That is the reach of the humble potato. Large tracts of land are cultivated in India in Punjab and elsewhere to grow potatoes for the multinational companies' chips market. According to FAO, a UN agency, per capita annual consumption of potato in the world is 33kg. That means that an average household of four persons may be consuming approximately 132 kg of potato every year. This probably excludes the family's visit to the MacDonald, Burger King, KFC etc. which use potatoes in a big way.

A famous comic story about potato typically goes like this: "one day potato messaged 'I love you' to ladyfinger. Ladyfinger snubbed him and also mocked him to be so fat whereas she was so slim and smart. Potato was crestfallen. He started befriending other vegetables and gave up on ladyfinger. Thus he came closer to cauliflower, peas, egg plant, radish, spinach etc. But ladyfinger could never find a match thereafter and is single even today." Can there be a handier and more adaptable food crop than this poor potato? Faced with people's agitation over bread shortage in France, Queen Mary Antoinette was immensely amused and blurted out, *"If they don't have bread, why don't they eat cake."* One wonders what would have she recommended the populace to eat if they were to complain of the scarcity of potatoes then! Perhaps she would have advised them to eat Sweet potato instead.

The lesson for our Agriculture mandarins is clear: encourage farmers and enable them to grow more potatoes and while doing so, learn from others' mistakes; don't forget the discomfiture of ladyfinger, which has already lost the fight. While we keep getting tears in our eyes whenever onion prices soar, the same amount of concern, responsiveness and empathy is missing on the part of policy planners in respect of potato. It is time to have a heart for this much maligned 'tuber' of all our happiness.

The 'Little' Bureaucracy
in Orwellian Times!

It is no mean feat to share your place of birth with a litterateur of the fame of George Orwell; add to that some class affinity – he was the son of a British official, it becomes a concoction of self-realization. This truth dawned upon me recently when I found Orwell to be a self-professed *lower-middle-upper* class. Now, many confused minds from the bureaucracy should contentedly adopt this brilliant ensemble and proclaim to the world that they belong to the *lower-middle-upper* bureaucracy i.e. self-determine one's rank in a system where the pecking order, euphemistically called the Grade Pay settles all claims to superior perks and status. The enigma gets sorted out by simple recourse to paraphrasing once standing in the scheme of things.

This realization is no less than a eureka moment as it would offer an easy escape route to a disturbed soul clamouring to find a place under the sun and would help it to sooth frayed nerves by banking on Orwellian elucidation. It is like attaining nirvana. Thus the protagonist would be suddenly catapulted into the hallowed confines of the exalted ones, thanks to the way shown by the Bihar-born English man. By relying on this characterization, the incumbent besides rewarding his alter ego would proffer a camouflaged social construct, namely evidence of the great clout of status – read caste, because the will and desire of status is as strong as that of the caste – consciousness that has an overriding influence in this country over all egalitarian pretensions. And the best thing is that the architect of this blasphemy cannot be accused of *double speak.*

But we must not forget that terms & conditions do apply. The espousal to adopt this new found equalizer for regaining the lost years has a fillip side – there is no material gain – as the person would have to be content with intangibles alone. Those in the lust of materialistic gains are ill advised to go for this nomenclature. They may not find it gratifying at all and would rightly accuse the preacher of this gospel to be leading them the garden path. But does one live for bread alone? What happened to all those lectures one attended on the art of living? The sublimity of life demands that we rise above the ephemeral trappings and look for staple for the soul. The exhortation is applicable, along with statutory warning, for the spiritually-oriented guys and girls only, so to say. This new dispensation has lot of merit – it transcends swiftly the meek-hearted to a new world of higher echelon – it sits you comfortably and smugly on a high pedestal from where you can also look down upon the lesser mortals with disdain. You may even keep them in fear & awe of your newly acquired standing as *lower-middle-upper* bureaucracy. Is it not a good bargain?

The question that should now be asked is how much good is really good? One does not need to attend discourses to give an answer. Perhaps we need to look for the general good or better still *the public interest* as perceived and determined by who else, 'us', the benefactors, and the beneficiaries as well – after all what do the poor folks down below know about their well being – as 'we the bureaucrats' have their best interests in our exalted head and somber heart.

Thus the public interest will be best served by appropriating to ourselves a certain status without which it would just not be possible to dole out the government munificence to the minions. Therefore, this much good should suffice for the present until something more ingenious by way of a 'public duty' comes along to further scale up our status in comparison with others in the rat race, for doing further 'good' to the poor public. Every new public service to be sustainable has to be linked to a step-up in our perks and perquisites; otherwise it becomes a self-effacing devise. The point that should not be lost sight of is that everything in this world makes sense only when it is relative – it becomes abstract and even meaningless without a reference point – and that is precisely what a hierarchy is all about. Once you have been able to posit yourself appropriately in that pecking order, you have done your *karma* and you can rest content that *moksha* would follow. Our salvation is in not in hankering after the worldly gains but in striving to look at the bigger picture and create a structure with us at the core of the maize; it eventually and collaterally brings in material gains as well.

Time is Money - Respect it!

The Brits moved their clock back by one hour on the first Saturday of March; they would readjust it on the last Saturday of October next by moving it one hour ahead. The difference between UK time and that of India therefore varies from four and a half hour to five and a half hours according to this arrangement. Why time is not attuned in our country? We endure stillness and remain oblivious of an important necessity. There is no reason for us to treat such proposition with contempt and do some serious thinking. It is not known if any recommendation has actually been made in the matter by any of those hundreds of committees that keep producing tons of reports every year, which incidentally nobody reads afterwards. Most of India is now brighter till late evening than couple of months ago; it is more lighted at 7 pm in the evening than it used to be at 5 pm in December. So why do not we fine-tune our watches, so as to make our time machine look more truthful? The logic and science of adjusting time with the movement of the earth contingent on the amount of sunlight it receives can hardly be rebutted, much less the advantages of such a move.

In a country of our expanse where sun sets almost at a difference of two hours from west to east, having more time zones is a given in the first place. While that is one policy matter begging decision, having at least time adjustment linked to sunlight is very much called for.An instance can be citedto illustrate how certain problems can be surmounted by such alteration.

Most of the eastern India, north-eastern states and Andaman groups of islands get the sun early and people over there plan their day accordingly. Government establishment in Andaman functions from 8.15 am to 4.45 pm. The guy in Port Blair would be up for his morning walk when a Dwarka resident (Gujarat) would still be far from any contemplation of devouring *khandavi* and would prefer to lie in bed to complete his most precious wee hours of sleep. The sun god would take two more hours to shine at the latter's window than in Port Blair. The reverse would be true that while the guy in Itanagar(Arunachal Pradesh) would have almost finished his dinner and planning to retire, his counterpart in Goa would have just begun relishing the first sip of his favourite Goan Feni.

Offices are working in many parts of the country till after 6 pm. You may need to call around that time from Mumbai or Delhi, a guy in Mayabander or Ghatal, ever heard the names – why should you; our world revolves round Delhi, Bengaluru, Hyderabad and Mumbai – to give last minute directions on an important point before calling it a day. These are small towns in Andaman and West Bengal respectively. But the offices at these two locations have since long shut for the day and you cannot get an urgent matter attended to your satisfaction. If the two clocks were adjusted, you would have known when to make the last call. Conversely the fellow at Aizawl (Mizoram) may like to pass an urgent matter to a colleague in Pune during his first hour in the office but the Pune guy would still be brushing his teeth, a situation which may not strike the former guy who is already in office by then. These are not trivialities but real life situations and avoidable.Time is money and this is not a good way to manage our time.

At another level, it would also promote greater economic efficiency. People in some regions would wake up early in summer if the clock tells them it is 7 and not 5 am. Having risen early they would contribute more to the production cycle. On the other hand being told it is already 11 in the night and not 9 pm during winters, will have a more sobering effect on some people with many positive gains. Those travelling by air depending on which way time is altered would gain or lose time as the case may be. In this age of internet and satellite phones, we cannot be so neglectful of time management.

Our Nationalism, Their Nationalism

It is an interesting paradox that many of us indulge in huge anti-social activities without any qualm but adopt a very self-righteous posture when it comes to taking position with respect to some international issue or a foreign country. Espionage activities or helping another country at the cost of one's own country are easily recognizable as anti-national activities. However, our indulgence in anti-social activities such as corruption, profiteering, hoarding, adulteration etc. that strike at the foundations of a nation get blurred and not counted in the genre of anti-national activities. It is a fact that nationalism started taking roots in our country much later, compared to the European countries or even Japan or Korea. The heroic acts of martyrdom truly happened for the first time when some Indians started avenging the killings at Jallianwala Bagh and some other wanton acts of the British Indian Government. It is not really a matter of pride that stories of heroics are much less reflected in our history than the history of derring-do of their people by many other nations. This statement is not to undermine the intense patriotism displayed by many Indians from time to time from ordinary folks to defense personnel and men and women of great character, but to mirror on what is missing.

The paradox being referred here is to draw a contrast between indulging in corrupt (read anti-national) activities and not having the mental ability or maturity to raise a voice even where State action seemed to be suspect from international humanitarian angle. We may give example of some major international events that were opposed or even resisted by shades of public opinion in some other countries on humanitarian grounds. The disastrous Vietnam War was regularly resisted and protested against in USA. There is abundant literature written by American themselves exposing the excesses of Vietnam War and the culpability of American administration in that human tragedy; ditto for the nuclear bombing of Hiroshima and Nagasaki. There is sufficient literature available regarding American support to Mujahedeen during the Russian occupation of Afghanistan and creating the Frankenstein, Osama Bin Laden. The Iraqi invasion by America was similarly protested against by scores of people on American streets including some prominent intellectuals and well known Hollywood stars. The Falkland War started by Britain was severely criticized by many intellectuals at home. There would be many other instances where acts of intervention in foreign countries have been severely criticized not only by political opposition but also by thinking people of those countries.

Let us refer to Dr. StellanVinthagen, a Swedish academician who launched serious campaign against Bofors Deal. He went on to criticize his own country for what he called "perverse profit making and making money by exporting war". He launched picketing at the sight form where Bofors guns would be exported and also tried to forcibly stop the manufacturing. He was sent to jail. Lest we forget, despite many excesses of the Imperial Rule, there were many voices of reason in that country who were sympathetic to the Indian Cause and aired their views publicly. Any display of such internationalism would be considered no less than sacrilege in our country.

The contrast to the above would be our intervention in Bangladesh in 1971 or sending the peace keeping force to Sri Lanka in 1980s. These were bold steps, calculated to protect geo-political interests of India and definitely right from our perspective. But why the other voice was missing? Well-researched literature is available now, showing the blunders committed by the deployment of peace keeping force in Sri Lanka especially, the inadequate assessment of the local realities, the resultant loss of faith with both the parties; our longtime losses apart from the assassination of Rajiv Gandhi included the death of large number of Indian soldiers in those unknown hostile territories. Less contrary opinion is perhaps advanced about the war fought by India to liberate Bangladesh. Maybe, we were right there or did do no wrong. But the fact remains that in both these major international conflagrations where Indian forces were involved, no voice was raised then against the State action, unlike instances cited above. But more importantly, any such voice would have been fiercely targeted as traitor's voice; pointing any question mark on these moves would have invited the charge of treason. It is this intellectual immaturity that is the mainstream thinking.

Two illustrations can be cited for making the point clear. Recall dissenting voices of two leading writers/columnists. They have no ideological convergence but their views seemed to strangely converge on the issue of J&K, albeit with somewhat different outcomes. One, the lady was scathingly critical of the Indian forces and guilty of making politically incorrect statements; the other one, a prominent media person reacted more like in desperation. He has not ventured out into further indiscretion, and has been kind of let off. The other writer stands quite marginalized for holding her radical views. We may further stretch the self-destructiveness of such positions by referring to statements and some positive references made about the national leader of an adversarial neighboring country by two prominent Indian political personalities. These two senior leaders since then stand sidelined in the national political scenario.

So the lesson is clear. Avoid the risk of resorting to intellectual honesty or airing opinion that is politically incorrect.

The Romance of a Train Journey

That a train journey could be immensely enjoyable had evaporated from my consciousness until very recently. It happened on a Friday evening when I decided to travel from Dehradun to Delhi by Shatabdi Express. Occupying the last window seat gave me a vantage position inside the coach, without the fear of being watched by anybody. For company, there were families, kids and people of all ages happily talking and eating snacks etc. As the train started moving, the nature's bounty started unfolding outside. Soon there was this wonderful spectacle of the setting sun dancing behind the woods and its redness swiftly spreading over the horizon. It appeared as if the train was chasing the sun which looked equally enthusiastic about the game; the sun kept playing hide and seek behind the forested land area that was going around in a twirl.

While I was enjoying this beautiful scene, my reverie was broken by a mother's admonition to her child to open her mouth wider — how much wider I could not fathom, being seated behind, as was evident from the constant refrain — so that mom could force the food down the unwilling kid's gullet. Parents I guessed could be quite an annoying lot at times, which I could gather from the poor child's meek protestations. Meanwhile, the lady's father-in-law sitting in the next row had suddenly pushed the seat backward with a jerk and the child's plate was jolted out, throwing some stuff on the kid and the mother too. The woman apparently was not amused and advised the old man not to behave like a child. But the latest ruckus brought me back to my own world beyond the window as I started getting a unique sensation from the goings-on in the woods outside. The activities between the setting sun and the forest were getting frenetic. The sky had tuned into multiple bands of deep flaming orange; it looked surreal. Never been exposed to writing verses, but wonderstruck by the visual delight of this sky on fire, words started forming into my head and oozed out into a couplet: *"Shafq ki laali ko dekh kar hota hai ye guman/Rukhsar pe sajaa hai jaise sharm ka partov"* (looking at the redness of the setting sun, an imagination dawns/the cheeks of the beloved lady are aglow with blush)

It must be clearly stated that these words, howsoever infirm, were captured not in appreciation of a feminine beauty in the tradition of Urdu ghazal, but in admiration of Mother Nature which granted me all the glories of a very unusual evening. Gurudev Tagore had exclaimed, *"Clouds come floating into my life, no longer to carry rain or usher storm, but to add colour to my sunset sky"*.

It was around this time that the train reached a station where I found large number of *sadhus* and religious looking people. Instinctively, I started looking for the name of the place and found it — Haridwar. So these were devotees who were travelling to and fro the pilgrim city. By then it was dark and the view outside was getting impaired. The excitement having waned, I recoiled and tried to resurvey my surroundings. Though not in Gujarat, it was clear that business acumen had gripped UPwalas as powerfully as many deals were being loudly settled over the cell-phones across the coach by numerous anxious and at times harried voices through instructions, reprimands, exhortations èt al. Later when the train pulled up at Muzaffarnagar station, many bearded people were noticed sitting at the platform along with some *burqa*-clad women, waiting for trains. My mind instantly registered the phrase — from Haridwar to Muzaffarnagar — perhaps, because it reflected the rich cultural diversity of our country.

Train journey could definitely bring great experience to anybody who is interested in knowing about the social, physical, linguistic and cultural diversities of the country. Perhaps a more comprehensive and better experience would come by travelling in general compartment. Be that as it may, the fun and knowledge gained during train journey cannot be matched with other modes of transport as people get to spend more time together. Even friendships are struck while travelling in long distance trains some of which survive a long time; something not possible in a flight. In fact in a long distance journey, after the initial tension of settling down people start unwinding and unfolding, almost like having arrived at home with packed food, clothing etc. This leads to sharing of experiences, discussion on social and political issues and the like.

The social and cultural life of our country is regularly reflected in Hindi films. The train life is also captured on the celluloid from time to time in films like 'The Burning Train', 'Johar Mahmood in Goa' and many more and recently in *Jab we Met'*. However, they mostly have been in the genre of a peripheral treatment. Perhaps a creative director may envision a more gripping screenplay by attempting to weave an engaging story revolving around a long train journey, encapsulating the 'Idea of India' — the thread interlaced with the social mosaic of travellers, their joy & enjoyment, their trial & tribulations, their fears — all this captured in time & space along with a touchy human narrative. The plot can be made into an immensely watchable, exciting, romantic and emotional tale.

Goodness in Greens! A place in Maharashtra

How Much Good is Good?

Like 'to be or not to be', how much good is good, also begs for an answer. We keep wondering about our as also of other's attitude all the times. From the early childhood, young boys and girls of respectable families are told to be good human beings. The guidance is regarding attaining a certain set of conduct that is considered decent, orderly and compatible to the prevalent mores of the society. The refrain is to develop well-mannered ways of sitting, standing, talking, walking, eating, almost every aspect of personal manners. That was of course then. It was a simpler and generally less complicated life as community was closely knit that made enforcement easy and compliance more visible. Every member of the community was a good soldier who could effectively intervene or at least oversee and monitor what was going on – remember the uncles, aunties, *bhaiyaas*(brothers) and *didis*(sisters) of the locality who knew the youngsters by name along with parentage – and reported back to guardians any incongruity that was noticeable. The informal social control was very effective this way.

The nuclear family of today coupled with belief in highly inflated individualism does not permit such controls anymore and moral policing is abhorred. In fact, such a move today would be out of tune with times, would be resisted, resented and snubbed both by the wards as well by the possessive parents. Minding your business is the in-thing and it is not considered cool to poke your nose where it is not required. The *mohalla* (locality) and colony elders are fast losing their relevance in this scenario. But that is not the matter of concern here. We are trying to look at the bigger picture as they say.

We may try to see the limits of goodness as opposed to absence of goodness. It may perhaps be said that goodness is a constant in time and space, though its scope and application may be a variable. However, the goodness of convenience is something that we need to worry more because it is cleverly camouflaged. This self-centric attribute is not because of any lack of due diligence. Rather it is the result of very well-thought off, self-serving reasoning and a calculated move to focus on orchestrated promotion of one's avowed goodness. There are many well-known illustrations of propagandist goodness from our daily lives. But coming back to our original subject, the point to ponder is why should goodness be rationed? If it is a virtue, then why it should not be unhindered and unlimited?

To draw back from history, the unlimited goodness as a way of social and political life was practically demonstrated by none other than Mahatma Gandhi. His declaration that an eye for an eye would end up making the whole world blind and his constant exhortation to shun violence even at the gravest provocation, not only emanated from his unflinching faith in non-violence but it also emphasized following an optimistic and robust philosophy of human goodness. It was not an idealistic concept but one that was highly evolved for its time and caught the imagination of the people like nothing before.

It is though not easy to encapsulate the concept of goodness as it may appear different to different people based on their experiences, perceptions and predilections. It may be either for practical and worldly considerations as hinted earlier or just as a matter of perception that varies greatly from person to person. However, we need not leave the understanding of goodness to the world of abstract and try making some sense out of it and look at it more rationally. If fewer words could be relied upon to express goodness, especially as a social instrument, 'civility, care and concern' could best suffice. This phrase of three words conveys a lot. It postulates an idea of goodness at its best. It shows inter-dependence of humans on each other and tries to bind them in a mutually responsible behaviour. A caring society is the best society and how best can it reflect its decency but by etiquettes and good manners of its individual members. These traits generate camaraderie, goodwill and we-feeling among the people. It promotes community-mindedness and bonding that strengthen the social fabric. There could perhaps be a way to seek goodness in our deeds. By extension, there does not seem to be any limit on goodness. While trying to measure goodness on a scale may be a good idea, let us in the meanwhile not stop spreading it all around.

THE PERIL OF DOING
NOTHING

A Rare Site! Udaipur

Reviving Our Riparian Culture

India has a huge coastline running to 7516 KMs. It also has many large rivers flowing across the length and breadth of the country. The ancient Indians, especially of the peninsula were sea-farers and good in navigation. It enabled them to circumnavigate the East Asia and the Far East. They went far and wide and culturally colonized territories as far as Kampuchea, Malaysia, Indonesia, Sri Lanka, which all show markers of Indian culture. Then, we started neglecting the coastal navigation and gradually lost interaction with the sea. This not only cut down our cultural and economic exchange with the outside world but also got us over and done with the absorption of new technology from around the world. This resulted in Indians gradually losing the comparative advantage; we aggravated it by disconnecting with the inland rivers as well.

Rivers, the cradles of our civilization for centuries, are thoroughly abused today. They are used as dumping grounds for solid and liquid waste as untreated sewers are allowed in the rivers, causing huge contamination. On the other hand, reckless urbanization and large scale encroachment on the river banks have curtailed their course. Most rivers have shrunk in length and volume. This has implications for our long-term survival and maintenance of ecological balance, besides severely impairing rivers' navigability. As the population and the vehicular traffic keep escalating, there is tremendous pressure on our roads. Hence, the need to find new ways including diversion of some of the motorized traffic through inland waterways. This area of developmental planning has remained grossly neglected. So what could be done?

We must enliven the rivers. They must be brought back to life through active measures by checking pollution, with a very heavy hand. Diverting the course of rivers and encroachment on its banks should be curbed. Once the pollution process is reversed and river banks are freed from encroachments, and cleaning up and dredging is taken up, the drift of the river against its natural course of flow will gradually reduce, which will improve its draft, volume and carrying capacity.

We need active involvement of the masses. Let it become a peoples' movement. Therefore we need to create a mindset whereby people recognize the munificence of rivers as a life-giver and learn to respect it. The public education and awareness is therefore crucial for the success of any project for rejuvenating our rivers. There is need to create ownership of the program that will give it strength and sustenance.There has to be an institutional and legal framework to plan, supervise, monitor and implement renewal of the rivers. We must find ways for effective enforcement of the legal regime.

Water-sports are largely neglected in our country despite so much water all around. Some serious planning can be done to promote this sector. A case is made here that the revived rivers should be allowed to grow as hub of certain cultural and sporting activities. A country with such rich and diverse culture has so much to offer to the world and why not weave them around our rivers. This must be complemented and facilitated through development of river fronts with adequate open, walkable space around the rivers. Thus the barrier between the people and the rivers has to give way to an enabling environment of easy access. When people will connect to the rivers, they will develop affection and respect.

The rejuvenation of the Indian rivers will not only benefit economy by facilitating alternate mode of transportation and increased productivity. It will also help preserve and promote our natural habitats and ecology, and create cultural space for greater public interaction. Our policy planners must give serious thought to culturally assimilate rivers with the lives of the people, revitalize them and make them accessible and navigational.

The Cathedral, Goa- White Beauty and the Ease of Access

Improving the Urban Pedestrian Mobility

Pedestrianization of Indian public spaces is of supreme importance. It will give an orderly and pleasing look to our urban landscape besides promoting efficiency and comfort for the masses. The fallout of automobile revolution has been the clogging of our roads and disorderliness of public spaces. Until 1980s cars were limited in number, they did not choke the roads so much, and public spaces – never much respected in our country – had some semblance of order. It is a different story today. The number of vehicles has increased manifold and cities are bursting at the seams. Taking Delhi as an example, there are more vehicles registered in Delhi than the number of vehicles in Mumbai, Kolkata and Chennai taken together. But that does not mean that other cities are any better. In this scenario, where would the pedestrians be? She literally occupies the last position in the value-chain.

We all know the ill-effects of noise pollution and how it is adversely impacting the wellbeing of the citizens. A recent international study has confirmed that noise pollution actually increases the risk of heart attacks by 12%. Noise in our cities can be mostly attributed to vehicles and more particularly to the nefarious practice of honking. We also know that the motor vehicles greatly contribute to the atmospheric pollution. They also cause grave human tragedies resulting from accidents, forcing many families to undergo severe emotional distress and deep economic hardships. However, these machines cannot be wished away; neither there is possibility of their numbers getting restricted. With a highly consumerist culture and rising income levels of the Indian middle classes, there is no going back on the acquisition spree of our countrymen. Civil Lines and Mall Roads in most towns used to be the most walkable stretches but not anymore; they have become a casualty of the vehicular onslaught.

There is a scheme of the Central Government known as Urban Renewal Mission. Improving the public space is one area of urban governance crying for most immediate 'renewal'. Our monuments, markets, malls, parks et al have been taken over by motor vehicles. We must retrieve our urban landscape from this mindless acquisition and reverse the trend to promote a healthy future. If the quality of life has to improve in our urban centers, the vehicles have to stop. Imagine the fun and beauty of family outings in Sector 17, Chandigarh, Connaught Place in Delhi, Main Road in Pune or the Mall Road in Shimla without being bothered by constant honking and fear of being hurt by a careless driver. The joy of being at such places would increase manifold if one does not have to constantly look over the shoulder for a speeding vehicle or navigate through endless number of them parked in the most impossible situations. Multiplicity of vehicles and their raucous cacophony leads to a disorderly, un-aesthetic and hazardous living in public spaces and also kills the joy of a leisurely stroll around a market.

So what is the option? Regulation! We must regulate what we cannot dictate.

There is need to rethink about a public policy on this aspect of urban governance. It would start with planning, public education, implementation and enforcement. There may be many options. We may start by having restricted areas in every town and cities which should be out of bounds for vehicles on all days for certain hours – the time reserved for the foot-revellers and respected as such – and this should be very strictly enforced, nothing less than zero tolerance, with exceptions only for fire and ambulatory services. Such regulations may alternatively be on certain days of the week or staggered over the day for different pockets of a city's public spaces. As these are put in position, strengths or weaknesses of the system will gradually be known. We may then think of revamping or fine-tuning depending on the weight of the problem. Since the success of the program will depend largely on willing public participation, they should be encouraged to give their inputs during the planning stages and taken into confidence for developing public ownership. Community leaders, Residents and Market Associations, Professional and Social Clubs, Educational Institutions etc. need to be roped in as core stakeholders to create awareness about the need and then for the success of the scheme.

This would also necessitate providing certain facilities as removing something without providing alternate system would not make the initiative sustainable. Better public transport to places of importance, parking facilities, ferrying people from Park and Ride stations, etc. would provide an enabling environment. Rules then will have to be rigorously enforced including imposing severe penalty for bringing vehicles to no-vehicle zones or for wrong parking.

Our public spaces need to be rejuvenated by creating a feeling of uncluttered existence where people could congregate. Coming together of the people would encourage public rejoicings and community-mindedness. This would help in building bridges of understanding, promoting mutual respect, strengthening social bonding, building social capital and quality of life – elements that are badly needed for better and safer urban living. And this can only be achieved by making this necessary evil (motor vehicles) as less intrusive to our lives as possible.

India Gate, New Delhi- Can Pedestrian be the King?

A Pedestrianized Habitation, Bhuj

Urban Decay Needs to be Stopped

Filth and noise seem to be the two most distinct features of our urban life. We are already at the bottom on most parameters that determine development standards; all social indicators, or human development index as they call it, portray a dismal picture of the country. But our griminess takes the cake and it has only been increasing as city after city is literally going down the drain.

Where to start finding the fault? Are we inherently dirty by nature? That does not seem to be correct – Indians have traditionally been very conscious of personal hygiene – but cleanliness does not extend beyond the threshold of our homes and there lies the problem. The bigger picture is one of total inertia of the general will with regard to maintaining a decent civic life and disregard of the rule of law, which leads to a non-performing culture that takes pride in lineage alone; all privileges must emanate from birth and status and not from merit. It is this mindset that has given birth to a negligent deportment as the core and defining physiognomy of our city dweller.

It is disgusting to find somebody peeing on the roadside, people littering in public spaces and indulging in insane blaring of horns. The widespread smudge all around is most annoying. The other day while the India Gate sported multi-colour images and was the centre of a beautiful light and sound program on the 'keep India clean' campaign, paradoxically there was litter all around being spread by men and women of all ages. Our torpor for the world around us and indifference to the environment is prodigious. Only psychologists and psychiatrists may help in finding the reason behind such glaring apathy.

We are a people that have least concern for the 'other' being. We clean our homes and shops daily but do not hesitate in throwing the rubbish on the street. That is what is most pronounced in our collective psyche – not bothered for what happens outside our door. No wonder we find garbage at the best of places; it could be outside the most posh mall or cinema hall or a high-end super-rich villa. So there is no ownership. The world outside my house does not belong to me and therefore is not my concern. This is leading to the growth of an unlivable environment. Our cities are extremely dirty; they present a wretched picture of urban decay.

The other aspect about lack of civility concerns the cacophony that we have created all around us. Ours must be the most raucous existence in the world. And most of this noise arises by blaring horns. Honking is therefore the biggest source of noise in our cities and we are not worried. Unfortunately it has become a mass contagion that has overtaken the entire nation in torpor. It is highly uncivil behaviour and disgraceful to say the least, enormously exasperating and causes extreme discomfort to the person who is victim of such mindless assault. It is a major source of stress-related disorders in our cities besides being responsible for physical harm to the hearing capacity as the decibel level is generally much higher than the permissible limits. Thus we are forced to lead a guttural existence.

Since the number of humans and the automobiles is set to rise uncontrollably, the future consequences of the resultant upsurge in muckiness and discordant ruckus can be easily gauged. It has already reached a traumatic level and further escalation would only mean a doomed existence in the cities.

The twin malaise could well turn out to be the biggest handicap towards building civil cities. It is a major challenge to urban governance and it is time to intervene to make a difference. Focusing on this neglected area of public policy by building a people's movement through a sustained multi-media mass-awareness campaign, involving the community in a big way and adoption of zero tolerance to nuisance by effective implementation of civic regulations would help.

An Expressway like this! NH 17

Expressways in India

It was once famously remarked by a US President, *"it is not because America is rich that she has good roads, but because America has good roads that she is rich."* That maxim in a sense defines what went on as one of the elements of development paradigm in that country a century ago. The initial advantage of creating good road infrastructure was lost many decades ago due to lack of foresight and vision on the part of our planners. While we failed in connecting our vast swaths through a network of highways, we also neglected to provide mass rapid transport system to our speedily expanding urban conglomerates. Coming back to highways, even the late beginning in this sector at the end of last millennium has not ensured that this delayed task is compensated through concerted planning and execution. We follow the same old ways of doing things that lack quality and quantity - quantity in the sense of size, width, and futuristic carrying capacity of the roads etc. The progress is tardy and the process embroiled into myriad administrative, financial and legal imbroglios, causing time and cost-overruns. Most targets of expressways have remained unachieved and the distribution of such networks is also not equitable across the states.

The whole process of urbanisation is unthinkable without efficient network of quality roads - while the march to urbanisation remains unchecked, it is not supported by simultaneous growth of basic road infrastructure - leading to severe traffic bottle-necks. The development of several allied economic activities has therefore remained stunted, which would have got a fillip had good roads been also planned along with new townships, industrial estates, institutional areas and farming sites. The new expressways are also deficient in many ways, including problems such as their carrying capacity, traffic management, ingress and exit norms, lack of road-trauma care, absence of developed slip routes for slow-moving vehicles and ease of access for the vehicles of peripheral towns and cities. Traffic snarls are therefore common even on short stretches of highways everywhere.

It is clear that road infrastructure is highly capital intensive, returns low with long gestation period and therefore finding resources by the government to revamp it is daunting. The challenge is now sought to be met by resorting to partnering with private players who are willing to invest in expectation of a reasonable return on their investment. But Public Private Partnership (PPP) has not delivered the best outcomes so far as it has been suffering from the initial pangs as also by inept handling of such projects, most important being inadequacy of project appraisals before starting the project and lack of dedicated support from the authorities. The economic rationale of PPP is based on providing an efficient public service at a reasonable cost. Secondly, it is meant to ensure that the risk that is being transferred to the private player is appraised and spelt out in unambiguous terms for it to invest and operate with some certainty. The terms and conditions of the contract has to be therefore well-informed by financial and economic appraisal that preceded the project planning. Most problems are being faced today because of not finding those determinants and enforcing them through a transparent mechanism.

India has ambitions of becoming the third economic power of the world in two decades and she has the potential. But we are late already and cannot afford any further laxity. There are institutions that are looking after such planning and execution. They need to have a fresh approach for planning of the projects and to adhere to a rigorous time schedule for meeting the targets.

Deaths on Indian Roads

Indians are dying on roads in large numbers – the number at more than 100, 000 every year is probably far higher than any other country. Tragically almost 300 human lives are lost every day; 12 persons die every hour on our roads. This is besides the number of persons who get maimed and crippled for life, and those who are prevented for months from earning their livelihood owing to injuries; above all the prohibitive cost of hospitalisation, a strong reason that ruins or pushes many such families below the poverty line. Thus a man-made calamity is ruining the lives of tens of thousands of families every day, besides causing severe loss to the nation by loss of man-hours. Consequently both the human and economic cost of this tragic situation is very high. There could be a queer comparative in terms of probably lesser deaths occurring in the medieval world on account of wars and diseases than in road accidents today. Is this the downside of development that has resulted in more disposable income in the hands of some people and pushed so many more automobiles on the roads? Or, the result of inadequate road infrastructure tied with non-adherence to traffic rules by the motorists? We may also closely look at the inadequate medical and ambulatory services available on our highways.

Most of the deceased and injured are pedestrians who are victims of not only reckless driving but also casualty of utterly weak infrastructure on the roads. The modern machine has become a huge killer not only because it is speedier and mightier but more so because we do not follow tenets that are followed by highway/speedway users the world over, and for the reason that we have not evolved adequate safeguards against abusive use of roads. Unfortunately the sufferings and trauma undergone by families of accident victims is a continuous process in the absence of any sound social security net, and keeps lurking as melancholic shadow over their lives and could be very frightening.

We may begin by first highlighting our utter disregard for traffic rules as one of the contributing causes of road accidents. The lack of respect for law is evident every minute; the guile violator well-ensconced behind the inept arms of law and smug in his position knowing the low cost of violations, if any. We have neither evolved into a law-abiding citizenry nor allowed the development of an efficient, firm and reliable enforcement agency that could impose its writ on lawbreakers. The lack of awareness on the part of road-users coupled with disregard for rules has been compounded by weak enforcement of laws. The result is there for all to see – the hazardous driving on the roads is rampant, severely endangering the lives of other users.

The problem is worsened by existence of bad road infrastructures that are unable to carry the ever-increasing load. Then there is issue of inane road-engineering at many places including absence of appropriate right of way for arterial and slip-way movement of vehicles, which could help reduce the vulnerability of certain high density road interjections etc. Pedestrians and cyclists as always are the most ignored lot in this scheme of things. Besides, we have no regulation to ensure that car owners do not multiply their number before mandatorily earmarking land per car for parking space. Having more vehicles on roads than its carrying capacity means congestion and bad traffic, itself a reason of more accidents.

The other weakness is in the system of driving licence that can be very easily procured by anybody. There is no rigour involved in procuring a licence, which sometimes can be obtained through bribe. The licence-seekers are not exposed to lessons, effective training and orientation that could make them safe and reliable drivers having elementary knowledge of traffic rules. What instead we get is a bunch of bullies, unruly marauders who treat the roads as a battleground. Instilling road discipline among this section in particular and all road-users in general is therefore a challenge for law enforcers. This needs to be addressed by a combination of information education campaign and strict observance of rules ensuring zero tolerance of traffic violation.

Finally, we have the issue of the golden hour. It is an unfortunate truth that many lives are lost because we are unable to resuscitate them during the first hour after accident. It is well researched fact that more lives could be saved if accident victims were rushed to hospitals in time. The best way to do it to have the injured on board Advance Life Support Ambulances as early as possible so as to prevent blood loss and enable resuscitation in the first hour by a team of neurosurgeons, orthopedists and anesthetists etc. on way to hospitals. There are structural inadequacies in our systems that prevent rapid action due as much to lack of resources as to lack of imaginative planning by the State, which should now rely more and more on private partners. Examples of this are seen in down south by organisations like EMRI that provides very efficient ambulatory services in a number of states. Last but not the least, there could be a National Fund for the Accident Victims as an interim measure of Social Security for the hapless sufferers.

Ganga, Yamuna, Sarsawati – Life-givers in the Throes of Death

It is well documented that all ancient human civilisations developed along the rivers, Egyptian, Roman and Mesopotamian, and the oldest of them all, our own HarappanCivilisation (popularly known as Indus Valley Civilisation) prospered along the rivers of the Indian sub-continent. Scientists also tell us that the earliest living organism took life-form in water. So water has been a life-giver and rightly revered as such by humans from olden times. Today most of us take it as a given and do not give any serious thought about its conservation. But more alarming is crass and wide spread violation of its purity. Our rivers today are extremely polluted and filthy; they are dying due to our total disregard to their safety.

Prime Minister Vajpayee visited Port Blair in 1999 and attended a civic reception organised by the Municipal Council, then served by this writer as CEO. In his characteristic style Vajpayee moved his right hand in the air, closed his eyes and remarked, "water-water all the way, not a drop to drink"! Brilliant that he was, he could remarkably sense water shortage as the most important civic issue. But he could also convey the deep concern that even in the midst of water all around, portability of water was a distant dream.

It is no rocket science to understand what has been going on. Our industrial, commercial and domestic waste is being emptied in our rivers day in and day out, besides wanton constructions causing diversion of the river course – the most recent case of Srinagar as a case in point. The rivers are treated like huge garbage dumps and routinely filled with muck without any qualm. As a consequence, they have not only reduced in length and volume but are also choking with toxic effluents including lead, mercury, arsenic, human excreta, rotting corpses and what not. Our rivers are not good for even irrigating the agriculture fields what to talk of bathing and washing. The resultant health hazard may be easily guessed. More unfortunately some of the toxins are getting passed on from mothers to their new born.

We go around with our daily core without any worry of the harm we are inflicting upon our rivers by thoughtless activities. Typically it also reflects lack of respect for the law. We do not care if nobody is looking and also because the cost of violation is very low. There are provisions under the Water Act but enforcement is poor. Similarly there are Central and State Pollution Control Boards for penalising such violations but not of much consequence. The town civic bodies are just not equipped to perform their mandatory and discretionary duties of checking and stopping filth from being dumped in our rivers.

In sharp contrast to our Ganga, Yamuna, Kaveri and Godaveri, rivers of the developed world are very clean. Fifty years ago Thames was declared a dead river but today it is considered the cleanest river in the world and its pristine sparkling water is savored by millions. Is it possible for us to go near the Ganga in Kanpur or Yamuna in Delhi for an outing? Our rivers are dying and there is urgency to restore them to life before it is too late. It is also a matter of inter-generational equity. We have had our fill, what about the next generation? Are they not entitled to have their share of this natural resource?

We may recount some social factors responsible for the present state of affairs:

First, we abuse the same rivers that we pray before – just like we murder the same women (dowry deaths) whom we pray as *mata*. **Secondly**, while we have venerated the rivers for centuries we have failed to bring them closer to our life. The citizen and his river live two separate existences. **Thirdly**, there is no cultural assimilation of the river into the community life. No social and cultural events are held near the rivers unlike foreign lands where people gather near the rivers for festivities. **Fourthly**, there is no connect between the city-dweller and the river flowing by his home. The river has been reduced to a third class status, only used for emptying our drains, dumping our untreated waste and doing some occasional ritual obeisance. Devoid of any emotional attachment, abuse is hardly noticed. Thus our rivers lead an isolated existence away from the humdrum of our daily lives. **Fifthly**, there is fault in our urban design that does not integrate the river in the urban design structure or with the life of the people. We do not have easy access to the rivers in any of our cities. **Sixthly**, it is the law enforcement agencies that need to share the culpability for having totally failed in enforcing the law against pollution. And that brings us to the **final** point, namely the low cost of the violation of law that we are so much used to in our country.

Revival of our River Systems has to be effected through people's participation. It has to be a mass movement; until the community is awakened to the grave danger that our rivers are in, it would not be possible to reverse the tide of decay. When people will have access to the river (a well –developed River Front), they will develop attachment, affection and respect for the river and when they will start loving and respecting, they would stop abusing her. Let us make our rivers access-friendly through imaginative engineering and landscaped walkways, and make it sustainable by involving the populace though information education campaigns and mass awareness.

A Tidy River Front! Udaipur

Green and Clean! Ahmedabad

Public Spaces in our Cities

It is one of the distressing realities of urban India that increasingly the open public spaces are getting converted into enclosed stadia, sporting arena or shopping plazas. These were traditionally available earlier as neighborhood grounds in our towns and cities till few years ago but have shrunk since then at an alarmingly high pace. While the developed countries converted these into huge urban spaces for the use of the citizenry, the haphazard urban growth everywhere in our country has put so much pressure on land that not a sq. feet of land seems to be left out for any other purpose than commercial or exclusive uses. It has two negative effects. First, citizens have fewer spaces for mass collectivity and rejoicings that facilitate collective unwinding from hectic work life. Secondly, it leaves little scope for the poor to look for shared enjoyment anywhere outside their homes.

We can see that this is in sharp contrast to what they have done in the West and developed countries elsewhere. All major cities of the world have huge public spaces where people gather with their families and friends to celebrate national festivals, special events, victory marches or even hold intellectual or political protests. These spaces are adequately excluded from noise and vehicular pollution. People can rest in peace not having to look over their shoulders as to which approaching vehicle is going to knock them down. Conceptually Pedestrianisation of public spaces should be the first and foremost planning to improve quality of life and facilitate such hassle-free enjoyment.

There are many instances to show how negligent we have been in planning for this essential facility for the ordinary denizens. But one or two will suffice. The India Gate in Delhi was built by the British to honor 'their' soldiers. 'Their' because though Indian, they died for the British empire during its colonial wars worldwide. It is a huge public space today but unfortunately the only one in Delhi. Similarly the Gateway of India in Mumbai that witnesses huge public gatherings was built by the British to commemorate the triumphant arrival of their monarch with all pomp and show to their conquered colony. Be that as it may, both these monuments however are very difficult to access by the ordinary mortals as one has to criss-cross through maize of traffic snarls. Pedestrian has no dignity in general in our country and much less in such places. At the same time we may also note that these two great Indian cities have not seen any monument of such gigantic proportion since what the Brits made.

One of the key challenges of global urban planning is to preserve structures and sites that promote identity and continuity of a place. Preserving the cultural landscape can help generate civic pride and foster a sense of empowerment, besides affording opportunities for cultural tourism, which is catching up fast in the international tourism market. It is needless to emphasize that collective gatherings – not talking of the individual groups of picnickers in parks or gardens – tend to promote solidarity and community belongingness.

It is observed that public congregations encourage people to be more communicative. The mere friendly presence of people of all age groups and backgrounds is confidence-generating, besides adding color and zest to the atmosphere. Such gatherings are conducive to building social participation. This in turn increases civic involvement. It also generates awareness and affinity for preservation of cultural heritage, which in turn promotes social cohesion. It is unfortunate that this vision has remained missing from our urban planning for the last six decades to the extent that even while planning for new townships and sub-cities where large tracks of lands have been acquired, no thinking is given to planning public spaces. It will be a toll order to think of London, Munich, Venice and Rome. Let us look at some other experiences elsewhere.

Singapore has increasingly included conservation of its urban fabric as an important part of its strategic planning with a new focus on place-identity, for developing Singapore into 'a dynamic, distinctive, and delightful city'. This plan was considered as an opportunity to engage a wide range of stakeholders in communities. The public is invited to share and discuss ideas and possibilities of how cultural heritage assets in their neighborhoods can be enhanced and retained. 'Communities in Bloom', Canada fosters friendly cooperation between communities to beautify their civic spaces. They organize competitions on issues such as tidiness, environmental awareness, community involvement, heritage conservation, urban forestry etc.

'Swindon Civic Trust', England declares its aim as improving the quality of new and historic buildings, and to help improve the general quality of urban life. The projects of 'Civic Exchange', Hong Kong include holding 'International Coastal Cleanup' for preservation of marine life, 'Clean Harbor-Aberdeen Project' (CHAP) for creating a sustainable and community-based initiative to attack problems such as air quality monitoring, climate change issues and conservation of energy; 'Central Park' for greening the city; and 'Students Internship Program' for undergraduates and postgraduates for promotion of civic concerns etc.

Examples can be multiplied by citing literature and pictures from world over showing how beautifully they have designed their public spaces that are aesthetically vibrant, free from clutter and conveniently accessible to the citizens. Rypkema in 'Celebrating our Urban Heritage - Globalization, Urban Heritage and the 21st Century' was not far from the mark while affirming Five Senses of Competitive Cities that included: the Sense of Place, the Sense of Identity, the Sense of Evolution, the Sense of Ownership, and the Sense of Community, to be developed through community engagement. We may try to learn from any of these models and fine tune it to our specific circumstances and needs.

An Open Playground, Goa

Free Access, Goa

A Non-conformist View
of Architecture

Passing along the highways and city streets, we see many big and small buildings. Some impress us, some do not. But certain structures actually put us off – one starts wondering as to why they came to be there in the first place. Many such landmark buildings can be named in our metro cities, but in this column let us talk of some in Delhi. For instance think of the two well-known Delhi buildings that will not fail to amuse you every time you happen to pass by them. If you look at the Vikas Minar and then at a structure called School of Planning & Architecture, interestingly both face each other – as if in unison they want to record and announce to the world their competitive monstrosity. Their shared objective in terms of functionality is apparent from their somewhat related public purpose and avowed usage. Vikas Minar was meant to be the headquarters of Delhi Development Authority – the contrast between the look and purpose of this building could not be more revealing – the organisation that created this ugly edifice has been ironically entrusted with the task of construction and expected to be in the vanguard of urban planning and infrastructure development in Delhi. The building is unattractive, appearing suddenly and rising incongruously sky wise from nowhere, and then standing arrogantly at an inappropriate position without any connect to the surroundings. With a structure like this how could one inspire confidence in the planned aesthetic development of Delhi's skyline? No wonder the quality of DDA housing projects has been the butt of ridicule in Delhi.

The other one, School of Planning and Architecture is even more extraordinary – it seems to have every element of a decadent design that an institution connected with study of architecture should have avoided. It is amazing how and why such façade of a building was ever conceived, an anti-thesis of everything that a good architecture should integrate and transmit. The building looks gloomy, lackluster, decrepit and uninspiring. It could have been better utilised as a consumer court, or as office of an enquiry commission or any other purpose except school of planning and architecture. Perhaps it was meant to amuse, surprise, shock and entertain. There are many other buildings vying for similar distinction like the Police Headquarters, Bikrikar Bhawan, PyareLal Bhawan etc. near ITO but the inverse distinction among all these must go to Shastri Bhawan in New Delhi.

Truly speaking these structures have altered the meaning of architecture itself. Architecture is meant to concern with durability, utility and beauty. While in the absence of information and data, nothing can be said about the first two elements, beauty is a huge casualty in these buildings. The planners could have saved the ignominy of these buildings by simply following the design of the oldest of them all namely the Revenue Building (IRS Hqrs.), which looks attractive and subtle in its expanse. The simple principle that could have been followed was to copy the best if you cannot innovate.

Becker, Lutyens, Corbusier, Stein, Christopher Charles, Claude Batley and others showed rare sensitivity in erecting some of those well-known structures than the indigenous geniuses responsible for the buildings referred above. Of course, we have famous Indian luminaries of architecture like, Charles Correa, Achyut Kanvinde, B.V. Doshi, Gautam Bhatia, Hafiz Contractor, Himanshu Parikh and so on whose contributions are immense. Architectural edifices take shape not in isolation but lie deeply embedded in the social context and the surroundings. They should reflect energy, feel and persona of the occupant or express purposefulness for which the structure is erected. Devoid of such essentiality, a structure becomes soulless. That is unfortunately what has happened with many of our modern buildings. Similar sacrilege has been committed in the name of architecture in other major cities.

Aesthetics is the most important element of designing a building. There are master pieces of architecture the world over and so also in our country, which elicit admiration and awe as also inspire the next generation practitioners to learn and replicate the experience without being imitative - those were fired by imagination and steered by vision to create. Beauty does not necessarily lie in the eyes of the beholder. A real beauty transcends and reveals itself to the world. Why a certain building attracts while the other annoys is the question we need to repeatedly put before the architects and planners. Why should we create pieces that do not relate to the surrounding, connect to the people around, and which fail to communicate?

Certain dreams are to die for and must be followed. Somebody needs to eat, drink, sleep, think and execute works like Howard Roark of 'The Fountainhead' before masterpieces of architecture could be created. The point is that chefs-d'oeuvre are not created every day. But at least do not produce pigmies in the name of modern architecture. Reimagining contemporary architectural practices from utilitarian point of view along with visualisation of aesthetic delicacy derived from the past and present for amalgamation in designs is a call worth taking. Since urban planning is a dynamic process and the modern pace is extraordinarily swift, the need for preservation is as strong as the unflinching commitment to innovation and imaginative experimentation with designs. By making this scientific art-form relate to the man (and woman) and his (her) environment we could perhaps achieve better results.

A View of the Fort with Sharp Angles and Expanse, Jaipur

Amazingly Harmonized! Himmatnagar Fort

Urbanization - An Aesthetic and Cultural Context

The process of urbanization is now considered a necessary and unavoidable result of economic growth and more so of industrialization. More than 52% population now lives in cities worldwide; this percentage is much higher in OECD countries and Europe ranging from 80-100%. The rest of the world is also moving in the same direction as cities are more efficient. They provide better infrastructure, transportation, health care, education and telecommunication etc. It is also a fact that urbanization comes at a cost, in terms of environment and natural resources. The process of urbanization therefore needs to be tempered with mitigating factors from the very beginning as shown by some of the western countries and also countries like Japan and Korea.

Urbanization does not only mean that the population is shifting its economic activities from the rural areas to the urban centers. It also means that people find in the cities ease of living in its entirety; better access by way of good road infrastructure and efficient public transport system, capable of moving huge population from one location to another with efficiency and reasonable comfort along with housing, health care services, educational facilities etc. But the most important element of a good urban living is the creation of an overall healthy environment in terms of good infrastructure, air quality, art and culture etc.

Some best practices undertaken by developed countries may be briefly touched for greater understanding. They have gone to develop the road infrastructure of high quality and extensively networked these with the interiors and outside of cities, the production centers and the hinterland. The areas around the roads are sought to be provided with green cover and landscaped. Inside the cities the roads are mandatorily provided with pedestrian walkways and convenient points of safe pedestrian crossing at suitable distances. The entire city planning is supported with green landscaping and street furniture, so as to create a mix of concrete and green public spaces where citizens can stop for a while and relax. It strengthens community orientation and a feeling of belongingness that goes to build the spirit of a city. The idea is to have the top surface of the roads, pavements and public spaces either concretised or with grass top. This helps in preventing spreading of dust from open earth surface. The ease of safe walking is necessary for developing an efficient public transport system. This means that after a commuter has completed his Metro/ BRT/Bus journey, he or she may well complete the remainder journey by walking on foot to the workplace, market, hospital or home.

Urban centers necessarily have to provide solid and liquid waste management, which includes collection, transportation and disposal in appropriate manners. A good handling of this aspect ensures that the urban space is free from litter and is well-sanitised. The same policies are extended to keep the water bodies around the city cleaned and sanitised including the river running through the city, if you have one. Having fair amount of plantations around the road side, the public spaces and important facilities is another important feature in urban planning. All this helps in creating a healthy environment and a city ambience to the urban space. The regulations are covered through Building Code and Bylaws that deal with not only floor area index and the limit on how much can be built but also other details relating to mandatory provisions of safety issues, symmetry, dimension, height, purpose of constructions etc. All this facilitates architectural uniformity, aesthetics in urban planning, promoting environmental concerns, optimising public services and so on.

Extensive use of private modes of transport clutters the city space besides causing pollution, noise, congestion and traffic-related accidents. These negativities are sought to be addressed by substituting private vehicles with public vehicles. So the best cities of the world are those which have efficient and safe public transport system. The underground network of city rails, variously known as metro, subway etc. are the best transportation mode provided they are efficiently managed, are punctual and well-connected to residential and commercial areas. This automatically reduces public dependence on personal vehicles and is thus able to handle congestion etc besides bringing efficiency. Urban centers require concentration of many other services, which need to be planned in great detail from the beginning - it is absence of this advance planning and their meticulous execution that leads to haphazard unplanned growth, crowding, and shabby surroundings of our cities.

While summing up, we may add that cities are not only concrete, steel and glass but the soul and spirit of that urban conglomerate as well. It is this element that is missing from our urban landscape across the country. And this is not something which can be engineered in months. It grows in many years through bonding and community participation. This contribution to quality of life of a city is as much from the hardware as from the software - unfortunately we are grossly deficient in soft skills - civility, care and concern, i.e. a general good etiquette towards others, women in particular and strangers in general. So besides investing in urban infrastructure, we also need to cultivate this trait in the younger citizens from early childhood through value education, good upbringing and training.

Right of Way - How Real is that?

Public Policy often embraces a debate on rights versus entitlements. While the argument may continue, there need not be any exception for a person to be able to walk on a street both as matter of right and entitlement. The courts might someday determine that the Right to Life guaranteed under Article 21 – that includes the right to live with dignity as interpreted by the apex court – cannot be comprehensive without the enjoyment of a fundamental facility, namely an enabling environment for a pedestrian to walk or cycle on a street. But waiting for that dispensation either from the court or from God is neither pragmatic nor desirable.

The urban planners in India are not yet serious about this very fundamental issue for ensuring good quality of life. A number of recent visitors from the other Continent spoke about the turnaround in quality of urban life through provisioning of special cycle tracks and walking trails along the major streets of metro cities. It has cured the woes of pedestrians to a considerable extent in those cities. Recently Janette Sadik-Khan, New York City Transport Commissioner on a visit to India spoke of making the pedestrian 'the king of the road'. That was remarkable and could become the *mantra* of our traffic despairs in big cities. Our cities and more particularly the metros are in dire need of walking space for its burgeoning population as neither the private nor the public transport or the two in tandem can provide the answer. Every single vehicle that is added to the road further reduces the latter's usability for the pedestrians and increases the travel time with enhanced chances of accidents – fatality on Indian roads is among the highest in the world. The option is to have an efficient public transport system that would ensure lesser number of private automobiles. But more importantly it calls for facilitating people's foot movement along the transport hubs, e.g. metro stations, railway stations, major bus stations and around the business districts. That should be considered to be the safest and cheapest means of public transport as also convenient, eco-friendly and health-promoting.

Taking Delhi as illustration that has the maximum number of vehicles in the country, it is at least lucky to have developed a good metro network that is expanding steadily and likely to cross 300 stations by the end of Phase III. But that is not the panacea. This infrastructure needs to be complemented by innovative and advanced urban mobility planning that takes care of commuters who would want to complete the remainder journey by foot. Personal car is found to be convenient from many angles; using it regularly is also habit forming. Asking a person to leave the car at home is not easy as it amounts to weaning him away from a habituated convenient facility. We therefore, have the prerequisite to provide good quality safe network of footpaths all along the transport centers. Having this substructure in position would encourage people to strut along the residual journey after utilising the metro/buses as the main staple.

Guaranteeing the convenience of walking from and to office, home, markets, stations, public places, hospitals, courts, entertainment centers etc. is essential for any efficient urban transport planning. That is possible only through a good and safe network of pavements. People would not leave their cars and take metro or the city-bus unless they have these at convenient points from their homes or places of work. So while the availability of the public transport is one issue, equally important is for a person to be able to reach there without depending on a second rung of transport e.g. auto rickshaw, cycle rickshaw, Tonga, whatever. Finding this missing link and shunning dependence on the second tier of transport through an extensive network of pavements is the task.

Pedestrianisation of public spaces is another area of public policy that has not been attended to by the urban planners. We have the tendency to reach by car the very last step of our destination; walking is generally abhorred but is as much avoided for being unsafe. Every market, monument, park and entertainment area is always choked with vehicles of all variety. The march to modernity of our cities gets badly hampered by this lack of perspective. Swift change over to multi-storied underground parking at such sites and strict regulation of unauthorised parking backed with charging hefty fines is essential for bringing in semblance of order at our public spaces.

Our cities have grown beyond their capacity without commensurate growth in urban infrastructure, the worst being creaking urban mobility. It gives a chaotic look to our public spaces, shorn of modern mien. It very adversely affects the quality of life, besides being economically inefficient and culturally retrograde. The need for change was never more pronounced. But adoption of new ways of life is generally as difficult as adoption of new technology or fresh technique of doing things. Change is often resisted or just ignored.

It is going to take time to convince people about the positive result by switching over from one mode of transport that they are used to and find more reliable, to another that is not in their control and hence in their perception less compliant. Their apprehension would come to rest only gradually and through experience. It is here that the car owners as also the others need substantive infrastructure to be motivated to adopt the change. The upgradation in urban mobility is essentially and inseparably linked to safer cycling and walking facilities in and around public places.

LEGALLY SPEAKING

The Victims of Crime

It is easy to take sides and we all keep doing it in different situations and at various moments in life. Human defense mechanism provides this therapy not only as a corporeal crutch to the weary body but also as a psychosomatic sustenance to the tormented mind. This rescue, soothing and healing for a brief moment is at certain cost though. We tend to forget that fairness is sacrificed in the process. The circumstances of victims of crime soon after the initial euphoria die down falls in this category. The victims fall into oblivion and are left to fend for themselves. Let us look at the scenario.

Special dispensation to prisoners with the avowed objective of reformation and rehabilitation is followed as a matter of state policy. No one in his right senses will grudge the rehabilitative and reformatory aspects of criminal justice system. It is, however about keeping the balance between the related segments that the system appears to be heavily faulted and biased towards the criminals alone. Typically the criminal justice system includes the police, the judiciary, the prosecution, and the parties to the crime; most importantly its victims. But the last mentioned is the least talked about and lesser cared about category in our society today. It is fashionable and politically correct to shower your compassion on the prisoners as it sounds humane, is socially more rewarding and sure to give the protagonist instant recognition as civil libertarian – same adulation not assured if you were to speak about the other (victim) party. That kind of adoration has yet not passed the muster for pleaders of the rights of victims of crime. The persons/families who have been wronged are neglected and forgotten. We are facing the same self-righteous approach as would generally for example permeates the subject of right to freedom of expression in absolute terms without mincing a word about certain social obligations related to that commitment. This is selective mass amnesia, duplicitous, deplorable and a matter of concern.

Victims are at the core of the criminal justice system and should therefore constitute its *raison de etré* but they are more often than not on the periphery and lose their relevance soon after the criminal is put behind bars. We agree that not all crimes are the result of criminal mind. It is possible that some offenders may get reformed and get absorbed as productive members of the society and that should be followed in the right spirit. What however one finds amazing is almost a clichéd and habituated response to play to the gallery by ludicrous appeasement of the prisoners alone without caring for the sensibility of the affected (harmed) person. This lopsided and biased attitude militates against the interests of victims of crime.

This is clearly visible when the entire weight of the establishment moves to an obsessive rehabilitation program of the prisoner in a sanctimonious and an exceedingly partial manner, impairing the psychological well-being of the victim. We need to debate. Would we be able to reform the depraved beast who raped a child or the brutal killer of a three year old kid or an infirm older woman? Coming across stories of reformation of dreaded criminals told with much élan and smugness by some of our benevolent rehabilitators may be chic but not really inspiring. Just pause to ask them what attempt has been made to follow the lives of the recipient of the criminal's lust/crime or to track the current status of those unfortunate wounded families. The advocate would perhaps be amazed that there could be even a perspective like this. He/she would rather be astonished at such silly conundrum. Most likely the reformist will have no clue to that query because the action in the meanwhile has shifted where there is flashlight. But there is a shadow area as well. The victims of crime do not have a voice; the system is skewed. Such facetious approach is causing collateral damage to dependents. We need to ask questions like what happened to the injured party. How is the family coping? Have they been able to piece together their ruined life? The society incongruously switches sides and in an atypical way transcends its loyalty to the perpetrators who are publicly felicitated in choreographed functions in the presence of page 3 personas. They are written about and shine in the glare of media.

On the other hand, apart from receiving legal aid from the State, there is no good compensation package made available to the victims by the Society, which nourishes and fattens the same persons who are the reason behind victims' sorrow. We hear regularly the story of bigwigs coming out of jails on parole for family weddings, medical reasons etc. But the victim does not have any such luck because there is no machinery for advancing his cause or espouse the enforcement of his rights. This is nothing but circumvention of a social objective to the total exclusion of the other party, who suffered at the hands of these state guests.

The end result is that while the doer is having it cozy in the Rehab (Jail), the victim or her family is cooling her heels forsaken by an insensitive world. On this fast moving Earth life has stopped in its tracks for them. They have been thrown in a listless trajectory. The pain felt by victims by this negligence must be as intense as the damage suffered at the hands of the criminals. Victims face financial hardship, feel disenfranchised, isolated and demoralized by the indifference of an uncaring society that sometimes make them feel as if they chose to be victim or were partly responsible for their woes. The rights of the wrong-doers are vigorously pursued and protected; same cannot be said about the victims of crime who wait to be heard and helped. We need to take an empathetic view of the situation and recognize the trauma and pain of the victims. A victim once remarked, "all I want is to be treated as good as a criminal in the criminal justice system". Their rehabilitation should be equally important for us.

Context, Size and Enforcement - An Issue of the Legal Regime

The delay in our legal procedures, more squarely the proverbial quagmire of court schedules and endless deferred dates are good to break any litigant's nerves. The cases drag for years, sometimes over two-three decades. L.N.Mishra murder case was decided recently in the fortieth year. Property disputes are settled by the time the main parties to the case are dead, sometimes even without legal heirs. This amounts to denial of justice. Added to that is the increasing cost of litigation, shoddy environment at least in the district courts, and prevalence of corrupt practices etc. But in this discussion, we may focus on a different issue, yet not really disengaged from the conditions mentioned above, namely, the weak legal regimen in our country, from the point of view of care, respect and concern for law and its weak enforcement.

The legal régime to begin with, as an inheritance from the colonial rule, is entirely constructed in a foreign language, is highly punctuated and verbose and complicated for ordinary folks to comprehend, let alone the distant likelihood of inferring or deducing any meaning from it. The syntax of 'subject to' and 'provided that', 'provided further that', 'notwithstanding', 'herein after' and thousand other such exclamations are in vogue that cannot be said to be even plain English. It does not help that literacy in general and legal literacy in particular is still low in the country. The task is then left to various players, some scrupulous, some not so, who understand and capable of interpreting the court lingo and have the forte to stand up between the four walls of law and the litigants. Typically this has fashioned a stratified, opaque and omniscient institution that is as inaccessible as it is irresponsive. It is not to say that we do not have good laws; in fact we have many. But they are very little understood and even lesser followed.

There is plethora of laws in our country, in fact a bit too many, and we continue to make couple of them every year. There seems to be an unusual belief that every problem can be addressed by making a law around it. There is no other demand in the public domain that is so vociferously and strongly put forward as that of making laws about a certain thing. In fact most political debates today are based on what should be the next set of laws – as if the new law being envisaged will cure the malaise in question like a magic wand. The result is that we perhaps have the dubious distinction of being a country with maximum number of laws with minimum degree of compliance.

Despite making huge exertions for making laws, we have not shown the desired concern for implementing them through institutional support. In the hurry to make laws, we tend to ignore the imperative of having in place a device that would facilitate their implementation. It is not surprising that many of our laws are lying frozen while the society suffers. The mechanism of implementation has to be comprehensive, i.e. informed by intelligent appreciation of what works, planning for it and putting it in position.

Next aspect in that loop is what we call enforcement of law. This is the weakest link in the chain due to various factors but most important and equally deplorable due to the wide spread disease of corruption that pervades, especially in the realm of regulatory and civic laws. Compliance is missing because a person or an institution easily gets away with violations at a low cost. The thriving industry of bribery ensures that enforcement never becomes a threat for those with deep pockets. The diversion of revenue through this process, a matter of grave concern in itself, is colossal but more importantly it promotes a conniving and acquiescent society that flourishes on circumventing the law through illicit means. Interestingly, the cost theory applies to both – the violators and the enforcers. Since the possibility of getting caught is minimal, the violators are not risk-averse. The enforcers are also risk-takers as the possibility of getting caught in the process of taking bribe is very remote. Thus, both are enjoying in a low cost scenario. The need is to raise the bar of cost for both, so that deterrence becomes robust. We have seen how the UK ombudsmen are effectual – their punishment is instant and hence sobering.

From Singapore to Japan and Korea to the Western countries, they have been able to break these jinx long years ago but we are lagging behind very badly. It is holding back our country from progress. We cannot be called a modern nation in the absence of respect for law and its effective enforcement. It is time we make a serious plan to do that. We sum up by quoting Pablo Picasso, *"Our goals can only be reached through a vehicle of a plan, in which we must fervently believe and upon which we must vigorously act. There is no other route to successes".*

Visibility versus Efficacy – A Case of Our Legal Régime

The legal regime is in a huge paradox. We are extremely poor in observance of laws but we have plenty of them. Laws in our country are hydra-headed, controlling, regulating, stifling, stunting and impeding most entrepreneurial energies, responsive governance and reforms. Because of the colonial nature and legacy of these laws, the State is in a position to intervene in any act of the citizen, and it can find a perfectly legal method to do so – there are multiple laws on every aspect of our life. On the other hand, if a person decides not to follow certain law or many laws, he/she can do it with equal ease and remarkable circumvention. So, laws are everywhere and intrusive but they are hardly effective. And since inefficiency breeds contempt they are not respected either. This is an unenviable spectacle for an acclaimed democracy.

So where is the inherent contradiction and why cannot it be detected and fixed? Some are underlined here for rightful appreciation of what has gone wrong.

First, in an overtly legal regime as that of India, the populace should have been and ought to be legally more literate. Just because general (language) literacy is low does not mean that there is no need of legal literacy ('law illiterate'!) and awareness. Neither the IT revolution nor the IIMs/IITs have been held back until the attainment of literacy, so legal literacy should not wait for general literacy, rather should go along with that. This is more about awareness of law and not about remembering their finer nuances, court rulings or citations. We must remember that there are several medical professionals who consume tobacco, despite being literate and knowledgeable but because they are not aware or awakened.

Secondly, but extending the same logic slightly differently, if 'ignorance of law is no excuse', then should not the ordinary citizen have the basic understanding of the law of the country before she/he is expected to follow them, or charged of some violation on account of his 'indefensible' ignorance. It has been said that "to force a man to pay for the violation of his own liberty is indeed adding insult to injury". It is unfair on the part of the State to hold an unwary person responsible for an offence unless he has been foretold about the consequences of that action. Just keeping that warning in a statute book does not make it available to the citizen – he needs to be made aware of it through education.

Thirdly, those who lead the government must be the first to show the way. The government is looked at as the ideal employer; it is because of this that the government servants have certainty and surety of job conditions and various safeguards, including predetermined daily wages even for ordinary labour. Being so, it is the political and bureaucratic structure that should be in the vanguard of showing deep respect for law and caring to enforce it. But that is easier said than done because of deep political divisions in the ranks of political executives that form the establishment. This show and commitment has to begin by total prohibition on anybody from holding the position of a public servant in case a criminal case is registered against him, provided the charge sheet is filed in a court of law within the prescribed time, until he is cleared by the court of law from that charge. This is going beyond a jail term or even conviction.

Fourthly, our institutions must be made fully answerable but strong. This includes statutory and oversight bodies, regulatory entities and commissions. They should all be seen as important lawful wings of the governance machinery that is capable of delivering and taking action. How the Ganga would be cleaned if the authority responsible for it has no authority to enforce its writ? This is not like making ourselves overregulated but just to ensure that if we have an institution for a purpose it should be legally effective. Unfortunately the Commissions of Inquiry in our country have been a huge waste of time and public money. When the findings are finally arrived at, these are sent to some hidden shelf of the government archives without disclosure and/or follow-up action. There should be some amendment in law to make its recommendations enforceable in a time bound a manner, and as a safeguard the commission should not comprise of less than three persons of legal eminence. The idea is to convey to the general public through these exemplary methods that the giver of law (practically) is as serious in its observance as it expects them to be.

Fifthly, having set the house in order we must undertake a comprehensive review of all laws, both central and state. Many of these are in dire need of being scrapped – more law, more violation. Many are archaic and redundant and lead to confusion, evasion and corruption, making the legal regime vulnerable to unscrupulous exploitation. It was George Washington who said, *"Laws or ordinances unobserved, or partially attended to, had better never have been made"*, and Edmund Burke, *"Bad laws are the worst sort of tyranny"*. Let us end the tyranny and make the 'law our public conscience' as suggested by Thomas Hobbes.

Weaknesses of the Legal Regime

The delay in our legal procedures, more squarely the proverbial quagmire of court schedules, endless deferred dates, increasing cost of litigation, denial of justice, shoddy environment at least in the district courts, and prevalence of corrupt practices etc. are good to break anybody's nerves. But in this discussion, we plan to focus on a different issue, yet not truly disengaged from it, namely, the weak legal regimen in our country, from the point of view of care, respect and concern for law and its weak enforcement.

The régime to begin with, as an inheritance from the colonial rule, is entirely constructed in a foreign language, is highly punctuated and verbose and complicated for ordinary folks to comprehend, let alone the distant likelihood of inferring or deducing any meaning from it. The syntax of 'subject to' and 'provided that', 'provided further that', 'notwithstanding', 'herein after' and thousand other such exclamations are in vogue that cannot be said to be even plain English. It does not help that literacy in general and legal literacy in particular is still low in the country. The task is then left to various players, some scrupulous, some not so, who have the forte to stand up between the four walls of law and the litigants. Typically this has fashioned a stratified, opaque and omniscient institution that is as inaccessible as it is irresponsive. It is not to say that we do not have good laws; in fact we have many. But they are very little understood and even lesser followed.

There is plethora of laws in our country, in fact a bit too many, and we continue to make couple of them every year. There seems to be an unusual belief in our country that every problem can be addressed by making a law around it. There is no other demand in the public domain that is so vociferously and strongly put forward as that of making laws about a certain thing. In fact most political debates today are based on what should be the next set of laws – as if the new law being envisaged will cure the malaise in question like a magic wand. The result is that we perhaps have the dubious distinction of being a country with maximum number of laws with minimum degree of compliance.

Despite making huge exertions for making laws, we have not shown the desired concern for implementing and enforcing them through institutional support. In the hurry to make laws, we tend to ignore the imperative of having in place a mechanism that would facilitate their acceptance in society and eventual implementation. It is not surprising that many of our laws are lying frozen while the society suffers. The mechanism of implementation has to be comprehensive, i.e. informed by intelligent appreciation of what works, planning for it and putting it in position.

Next aspect in that loop is what we call enforcement of law. This is the weakest link in the chain due to various factors but most important and equally deplorable due to the wide spread disease of corruption that pervades, especially in the realm of regulatory and civic laws. Compliance is missing because a person or an institution easily gets away with violations at a low cost. The thriving industry of bribery ensures that enforcement never becomes a threat for those with deep pockets. The diversion of revenue through this process, a matter of grave concern in itself, is colossal but more importantly it promotes a conniving and acquiescent society that flourishes on circumventing the law through illicit means. Interestingly, the cost theory applies to both – the violators and the enforcers. Since the possibility of getting caught is minimal, the violators are not risk-averse. The enforcers are equally risk-takers as the possibility of getting caught in the process of taking bribe is very remote. Thus, both are enjoying in a low cost scenario. The need is to raise the bar of cost for both, so that deterrence becomes robust. We have seen how the UK ombudsmen are effectual – their punishment is instant that acts as a deterrent.

From Singapore to Japan and Korea to the Western countries, they have been able to break these jinx long years ago but we are lagging behind very badly. It is holding back our country from progress. We cannot be called a modern nation in the absence of respect for law and its effective enforcement. It is time we make a serious plan to do that.

Old Enough to Commit Crime, too Young for Punishment

The most degenerate, atrocious but youngest of Delhi's rapists was in the news this week for having been awarded glorious confinement of less than three years at a correction home — a place where he will get to indulge in all his juvenile exuberance and delinquencies with greater gusto, including bullying his juniors and harassing the keepers, and come out later as a more hardened criminal.

The spontaneous shame, sadness, anger and frustration felt by the people at the extreme brutality inflicted upon the girl has ebbed. But was that beastly crime the end of such violence against women? If the incidents reported in newspapers everyday are looked at, the answer is a resounding no. Daily stories of violence keep emanating from across the country.

Sensitive people individually and organisationally have taken up the fight against this horror and many have advocated dire punishments for curbing such crimes through stringent laws and summary trials; at the same time efforts are being made to develop sensibilities to the issue of crime against women and for creating awareness for changing the mindset of men. A debate is also on about the juvenile age to be brought down to 16, which has not found favour with votaries and activists of child rights. This aspect deserves our special attention, more particularly as the crimes committed by persons of this age group in recent times has acquired extreme brutality and depravity.

It's not clear why this demand is not being conceded or being given serious consideration. We must not allow this issue to become a turf war between the activists of women rights and child rights — that will not only be ludicrous but will also harm a serious social cause. More importantly, a person who commits such a horrendous crime is not a child anymore and should not be treated like one; by the act of his perversion he should be deemed to have invited normal criminal law upon himself. The maxim should be, if he is old enough to commit such crime, he is not young enough to be treated in accordance with child laws.

Even at the cost of repetition it needs to be reiterated that if the delinquent is old enough to nurture the thought (criminal intent) and relish the depraved enjoyment of such act, then he is not young enough to deserve leniency of law and therefore should also suffer the consequences of his adulthood wickedness. He is not entitled to seek double advantage of 'doing' an adult act and then claim to be a 'child'. It not only makes the law illogical and grossly unfair but also acts as double jeopardy for the victim of the crime who in this case suffered gruesomeness and untimely death at the hands of a 'child' who claims immunity on account of his age, manipulates the retributive process taking advantage of the lop-sided law and evades punishment. Thus the law as it exists is weighed heavily against the victim of such crimes.

We cannot have a just society unless the law is dynamic and adapts to the newer challenges and demands put on it by societal needs as also by those who constantly try to ransack it, i.e. the circumventors. The question that needs to be asked at this stage is why and when laws are made and for whom?

The common sense answer would be that they are made to establish social order, to make the individuals follow and adhere to societal norms for the good of the largest number. This demands different provisions at different times depending on changing circumstances and social mores. Clearly they are, therefore, made for protecting the society from criminal acts of criminal minds.

And perpetrators of crimes are not convicted on the basis of accusations or allegations but on hard evidence — there is little possibility of an innocent person being convicted, though he may remain in custody for a while during the trial — so the stance taken by some that it will adversely affect the rights of 'children' (juveniles) is devoid of merit.

Enough violations have happened destroying lives and families. How many more women have to endure such brutalities before the system relents? While the law relating to rape definitely needs to change, there is a strong case to change the law relating to the age of juvenile, especially for those involved in heinous crimes. We do not need to invent the wheel to do that.

There are many countries which have reduced the age of regular trial forced by seriousness of the increasing crime rate among juveniles. We, therefore, need to come out from this holier than thou position and adopt a more prudent approach to take the bull by the horn. The law has to be more responsive to the challenge being thrown by new typology of crime, symbolised by extreme viciousness, which cannot be tackled by soft peddling and mouthing platitude for rights of those who do not deserve it. It is time to jettison the ostrich like posture and call a spade a spade. Our society will be safer if such monsters are incarcerated for long years.

Mother Nature and
the Legal Culture

Concern for environment has fortunately acquired more recognition the world over and now in India too. The worry is however at a very nascent stage in India and that too mostly limited to paying lip service. In fact, it is generally fashionable in higher social circles to talk of protecting environment without going deeper into its causes and the possible solutions. The environmental pollution has spread over the last century, with severe damages to human life and habitat - from reckless industrialisation to spurt in automobiles to deforestation to contamination of rivers and aquifers etc. It has taken a huge toll - grave health hazard for humans, depletion of Ozone layer, global warming, severe threat to marine life etc. Our cultural festivals pay no regard to the need of nature and are no less responsible for adding to the air and water pollution. Added to our woes is our burgeoning population, institutional weaknesses and terribly weak compliance to the legal requirements.

India is facing similar situation today as the West faced almost hundred years ago; but we cannot wait for next hundred years. The West realised it much before, started taking corrective measures with newer technology, mass awareness and public involvement; their economic advancement and sound political and social structure facilitated remedial course.

The fundamental change has to begin by creating mass awareness to protection of nature. Public has to become the primary stakeholders not only for their own sake but also for inter-generational equity. Nothing less than a people' movement for regeneration of environment is the crying need of the day. This has to begin early and hence the need to have very special courses in school curricula creating sensitivity for environment and respect for its regulations, so that the young boys and girls imbibe the right values and develop stake in protecting environment. Let them be the eco-ambassadors to carry aloft the struggle during the next ten, fifteen years.

Our issue is not the non-existence of law; we have plethora of laws, perhaps more than any other country. The disturbing fact is that we do not allow its writ - it starts from our mindset, basically no respect or fear of law - because cost of violation is very low. Influencing the course of law is common as we are a country of VIPs. Our VIP-centric culture makes everything possible, from violation of law to getting scot-free after serious offences. Therefore, enforcement of law without fear and favour is a toll order in our country - the reverse happens only where a matter gets into the public domain through media discovery and the resultant public attention etc. But it does not mean that common people do not try to influence the law, in fact everybody does. So again, the issue of sensitization comes, that is to say that the citizenry has not learnt to live and abide by law for the larger good of the society. We as a nation need to train ourselves to play by the rule. An ethical awareness and commitment for following certain set of societal code has no substitute for the success of such environmental renewal.

Apart from legal recourse, persons/industry found involved in causing air and water pollution should be shamed publicly for creating deterrent effect. Public awareness and consciousness on the issue has to be from both positive and negative angles, i.e., for the cause and against the wrong-doers. This may be taken as the preparation time, like any cookery recipe. Once the social sanction and societal awareness is built up, technological innovation and absorption would have greater impact and implementation easier. The design and architecture of our planning cannot be replicated from some foreign model lock, stock and barrel. It has to be suited to the peculiarities of our country taking into consideration the levels of underdevelopment, poverty, illiteracy and lack of awareness (read dogged resistance to a civil behaviour) and democratic aspirations (read license).

Just as the legal framework, the institutional framework is also largely available in our country; there are many regulators and watchdogs; if anything, they sometime overlap and work at cross-purposes. But their non-existence is not our despair. Our worry is that they have become flab, bureaucratic and non-functional and they need to be energised and made to deliver. There is a Central Pollution Control Board and chain of these in every state, besides other government departments and agencies that are entrusted with the job of monitoring, regulating, controlling and punishing wrong-doers for environmental degradation. But that is not happening because our agencies are not put to the best use - many of these, with exceptions of course, have become parking lots for influential persons - as they are not equipped by skill or motivation to undertake such onerous task.

Lastly, not having any better option, we may think of having fast-track courts for this sector as well. Summary decision in cases of violations, appeals and award of punishment etc. may help in checking the rot and in establishing the rule of law, especially over the high and the mighty. We must not bequeath to the next generation, a world that is worse than what we inherited.

LIFE BEYOND
THE BORDERS

Asian Tigers have Shown the Way

The exceptional triumph and masterly stroke of the recent SAARC diplomacy in New Delhi, has been acclaimed and widely written about and we may move to other issues. Our attention may now rivet to group of countries, commonly clubbed as Asian Tigers but generally speaking not much in consideration in our scheme of things.

It is abundantly clear that the biggest focus of the new regime would be governance reforms. It may therefore, be in the fitness of things to lay weightage on finding the best partners around the world, for developing our infrastructure projects. While SAARC initiative must continue, it would be expedient and pragmatic to look beyond and be guided by pure economic sense rather than just the geo-political calculations. It is in this context that close cooperation with the East Asian countries is suggested as of great significance for urban renewal in the country.

Now looking at the Indian scenario, are our cities livable? The urban population that was 25.85 million (10.84%) in 1901 rose to 285 million (27.78%) in 2001. The last decadal growth has finally shown the changing scenario — while the rural population increased by 90.06 million, the urban population enlarged by 91 million and this might be the new irreversible process, i.e., urban population will increase more in coming decades. As per the latest census figures, 377 million people in India live in urban areas, which figure is higher than the combined population of USA and UK.

It is further estimated that this may swell to 550 million (42%) by 2030. Continued urbanisation, therefore, appears to be the inevitable process of economic development. Clearly the proportion of people living away from agricultural activities is rising as agriculture is not able to support them, triggering large scale migration to cities in search of livelihood and better living conditions. The burgeoning population has put severe pressure on existing infrastructure in the cities, causing housing shortage, water and power crisis, congestion, poor public transport, public health and waste disposal problems, environmental degradation, and severe strain on delivery of services like sanitation, health and education. Earlier, realising that our resources and skills were not commensurate to the task at hand for developing infrastructure projects in the country, we took resort to the PPP mode with some good result. Therefore, if we can get things done (public works) through Indian business houses, we should not be naïve not to get our infrastructure projects done by highly efficient, technically qualified and experienced agencies of these Asian Tigers who have revolutionised their own infrastructures. It is not that we have no collaboration with them but in comparison to their extra-ordinary success story, the partnership is much smaller in scale than it could or should be.

We have remained enamored too long with the West, perhaps due to historical reasons but also because of a sense of inferiority vis-à-vis our erstwhile rulers. So success stories from nearer home are found less inspiring and worth emulating than the *firangi* (slang for Western things) experiment; lest we forget, we have this deplorable weakness for the white skin that often determines our responses to various situations and demands. Thus, while we may have heard of Asian Miracle we refuse to be impressed. The Asian Tigers like Singapore, Hong Kong, South Korea and Taiwan showed how they could revamp their economy through rapid industrialisation and achieve parity with the Western countries in terms of generating national wealth and in raising all other indicators of human development. Leaving aside other aspects, we may just focus on how well they have changed their urban landscape and made their cities world-class. Let us agree that they did things differently and built up robust high-income economies through competitive advantage and export-led rapid strides with growth rate of GDP maintained at or above 7% to 8% per annum — Shiv Khera speaks of successful people doing things differently. Others in the league like Indonesia, Malaysia, Thailand, besides of course China and Japan showed similar grandiose growth. Why don't we learn to do things differently?

Summing up, our cities like our rivers present a pathetic picture of shabbiness and decay and in sharp contrast to the cities all around the developed world. No doubt, it is also a reflection of the general level of under-development that the country is faced with. Nevertheless, we have some pockets of excellence in every major metro and big city. Why we are not able to expand that distinct look to more areas of the urban sprawl. From roads to mass urban transport, to Railways, to water supply, to waste management and health services, our urban living desperately awaits improvement through appropriate technology, modified to suit our specific needs and finding the funds for the same. It is here that we may want to rely more on these countries. The fact remains that these nations transformed themselves through global value chain. The rich experience of Asian Tigers should be a huge inspiration for us and a resource that we have not tapped yet.

Uncle Sam Must Learn

The unipolar world is completely dominated by one super power but in ways that cannot be considered always worthy. The discordant voices from North Korea, Syria, Iran notwithstanding, the sweep of control is near total across the vast swaths of seven continents. Information is efficiently managed and controlled and sometimes viciously manipulated, like WMDs of George Bush. Apparent beginning was the policy of 'Regime Change' some years back by direct invasion and supplanting the local command structure and imposition of a friendlier establishment. But interventionist policy is there for half a century now and the political sanction behind that even older. So the action in Libya, Afghanistan and Iraq cannot be seen in isolation - it helped though, as these regimes were extremely oppressive, totalitarian and had lost legitimacy - but they were still internal matters of these countries. The threat is now on Syria and Iran, the former also a discredited regime but the same may not be said about Iran, which despite its alleged aberrations is a democratically elected government.

Historically, there are many firsts on the part of USA, in the range of international policing beyond the ambit of the world body, UNO. The controversial and one-sided solution of Palestine issue in association with the West in the 1940s and dropping of atom bombs couple of years later on hapless Japanese cities of Hiroshima and Nagasaki almost started the setting of a hegemonistic interventionist trend worldwide. The absolutely torturous and unjust Vietnam War has been a blot on the democratic ethos. That today it is attempted to be glossed over by professing apologies and meek explanations, does not reduce the ignominy of that adventure. We in India also got a feel of this threat looming large in the Indian Ocean, by the deployment of the Aircraft Carrier *USS Enterprise* by the Nixon Administration, popularly called as the 7th Fleet, during our conflict in the Eastern sector in 1971. It is another matter that the crisis was averted by the grit and determination of the then Indian Prime Minister.

Even much earlier there was systematic annihilation and wiping out of local ethnic population of Red Indians within their own country. Thus effective and deadly interventions have been a routine. The USA has supported dictatorial regimes world over including our own juvenile-delinquent neighbour, for protecting their geo-physical interests. It is also known that many monsters had been a creation of American policies, like the building up of *mujahedeens* in Afghanistan to fight the Russians. They forgot that riding a tiger is always risky; Hillary Clinton's snake-in-the-backyard-fame allusion equally applies to the USA. The dictum of the super-power is loud and clear - everything is fair in war - and no other country improved that strategy into an art form better than US. Many of these interventions have been achieved with collaboration of other Western powers or with their complicity.

It is a hugely ironic situation and not easy to explain. USA is the biggest contributor to the kitty of UN finances. We respect their commitment to democracy, liberty and humanitarian aid programs. Their's is a highly developed, vibrant, thriving and sound internal democracy that the world has a lot to learn from. The index of freedom is highly developed in that country with a chain of democratic institutions, which ensure individual freedom to the fullest even after 9/11. America has welcomed people from the world over and provided them wonderful opportunities to grow and enrich - it is the ultimate destination - the idea of the Great American Dream. No wonder it supports a huge Diaspora from every corner of the globe.

Therefore the paradox is all the more complex and difficult to explain. The essential problem is then with US foreign policy. Unquestionably, foreign policies are guided by interests of each country, which are paramount and competing; many constructive as also subversive activities also happen behind the façade of diplomatic finesse. All that is acceptable in accordance with international norms. What has, however, corrupted the system is the old cliché, 'white man's burden' that consciously or unconsciously America borrowed from its original mainland settlers and started enforcing on a hapless third world with added arrogance and vastly improved technology. The James Bond like action and his license to shoot and kill have been invoked with impunity and without concern to the systemic erosion of international laws. Would Obama be able to put America on a different course, is a million dollar question.

Do We Live in a More Peaceful World?

The world has come closer with new discoveries. Technology has made it possible to know about each other and communicate faster. The internet, cell phones and dish antennae have made it possible to connect with whatever is happening in any corner of the world at the click of a button. We keep hearing of turmoil like the Arab Spring, terrorism, military built-up around some regions, daily bomb blasts in Iraq and Afghanistan, crisis in Syria and Somalia, threat from North Korea – and about several other volatile pockets. They often generate fear and alarm about violation of human rights, worse loss of human lives. These are matters of genuine concern and rightly so. In fact we know a lot about the goings-on around the world and are apprehensive about nuclear conflagration, poisonous gases, bio-chemical wars etc. Thus armed with advanced knowledge of the world, we tend to carry the impression and even convinced that we are living in a dangerous and violent world. Not surprisingly, we call the present as the worst period, *kalyug* and apprehend the nearness of *kaal*(apocalypse). In reality the world today is much less violent than it used to be in the past centuries.

So let us make an outlandish statement that our generation lives in a safer world and try to see if that can be sustained by some arguments. Many would consider this bizarre. But there are cogent reasons behind making this unusual statement. The ancient and medieval world witnessed far too many unparalleled human catastrophes, from the times of the *Mahabharata*. Despite all the violence that we see around us, it is much less than what happened during innumerable battles of the ancient and medieval world. Let us remember the marauding and killing forces of Mongols and Huns. Everything perished that came in the way of the militaries of Halaku and Chengiz Khan, the Far-eastern marauders. Today's civilized continents, Europe and America had had thousand battles including the Crusades, the mighty battles of the Roman Empire, the Hundred Years War, the War of Roses, the Crimean Waretc., not to mention the battles fought for and against the French Revolution and last but not the least the two World Wars before moving forward. They witnessed the fallouts of the American War of Independence and the Civil War and the French Revolution. We cannot forget the brutal purges of the Stalinist era in the Soviet Russia. Even these paled into insignificance by the horrors of Nazi Germany under Hitler. We had Nero earlier and Mussolini later. Lest we forget, the Vietnam War and earlier to that the nuclear attacks at Nagasaki and Hiroshima by America were responsible for colossal loss of human lives. The two World Wars together led to the loss of no less than twenty million human lives. We may also respectfully remember all the heroic lives lost of the suppressed nationalities that fought for freedom from imperial yoke.

Nearer home, we may recall the death and destructions of hundreds of battles fought by the Kings and the Rajas of the yore, the ravages brought by the ruthless Afghan invaders, Ahmed Shah Abdali and Nadir Shah Durrani during the 18th century, retaliatory deaths in the aftermath of the suppression of the 1857 Uprising, and the untold killings and human misery of the Partition Era. China had its share in the Cultural Revolution, Bangladesh during its War of Liberation and Kampuchea during the Pol Pot regime. Looked at from this perspective, the horrors of wars have subsided to a great extent. The battles that ravaged in all parts of the world claimed hundreds of thousands of life every year. While scores died on the battle-fields, many more succumbed to the injuries due to lack of medical relief – a wounded soldier had less than 10% chance of surviving a wound received in the battle ground, let alone those with mortal disabilities.

Secondly, the diseases and epidemics took a huge toll of life. We may remember how villages after villages and towns after towns were laid waste by plagues and cholera that left vast swaths of habitation desolate for years and it was impossible to count the numbers of humans who perished like flies. Thirdly, in various parts of the world famine was as frequent as the annual floods and the two together devastated huge areas of land and destroyed massive population. The locusts completed the remaining task by destroying the crop and in aggravating the famine conditions. A word may also be said about various diseases that killed human beings routinely in the absence of medical facilities. There is no doubt that the advance in medical sciences has helped in preventing and controlling ailments in a big way and thereby save human lives. Perhaps the only factor that takes a huge toll of life today and which was not a threat in the earlier centuries is the accidental deaths or more precisely the deaths that occur due to vehicular accidents on roads. But barring this, which is not insignificant though, all other reasons were much stronger in the earlier times.

The world population has seen an unprecedented increase - manifold during the last one hundred years – and India is the best example. Ours may not be an Ode to Solitude but definitely a limerick to peace and security. There are inequalities, injustices and many other ills that we would desire to vanish. But what the present age brings to the world is not only promise of life, but also dignity as a gift of democracy. Let us avoid pessimism and embrace hopefulness and feel sanguine about the credo of the modern world – to live and let live. We may perhaps agree that humans today are living a more orderly and peaceful existence than ever before.

International Conflagration
or a Humanitarian Disaster

The portents over the West Asian sky are getting increasingly ominous. The piety associated with Ramadan and all the exhortations/injunctions to the faithful about striving for peace and harmony have failed to check or control the latest brand of marauders reminiscent of the violent campaigns of Attila the Hun and Mongol ruler Genghis Khan's incursions in ancient and medieval times respectively. IS is unleashing wanton killings, mayhem and indulging in fratricidal warfare. Massive assassinations and destructions are happening in Iraq and Afghanistan – there are several other conflict zones around the world that are dangerous and act as killing fields.

IS swears and lives by blood-letting. They have no patience for anything; let alone sitting across tables for negotiating terms of settlement. The militiamen are dreaded as fierce combatants who shoot before they talk. The world is watching this engulfing anarchy with awe, trepidation and concern, while blood flows all around without regard to the identity of persons, combatant or non-combatant, young, old, child or women. On the other hand the rulers of these territories unfortunately are as a general rule incompetent and tyrannical, which does not help the situation either.

Unemployment, run-away inflation, destruction of infrastructure in the war-ravaged cities, the desolateness and infertility of vast swathes of land, scarcity of basic essentials - goods and services, and the overall social and economic distress have made the populace of these countries weak, chauvinistic, xenophobic and vulnerable to all types of malfeasance. But those are still the symptoms, the problem lies much deeper.

Whether it were the *mujahedeen* fighting Russian occupation of Afghanistan then or several other outfits since then, conceived, created, reared, trained, armed and pressed into service by Super Powers for serving their interest, or various overt or covert activities carried out under the aegis of power politics or simply for politico-economic domination, the trail of evidence available through academic writings and well researched books give the most wretched story of worst manipulation of the weak by the strong. These have had fatal consequences; the trail of devastation is far too evident.

This gloomy scenario has an analogy to the 'chicken and egg story', which should make us pause and think. Are these the bad boys who started it, or were they goaded by the good boys into doing this? The theory of causation has thus to be relied upon for seeking the reasons behind the imbroglio. There are lessons in history. We must not forget that foreign rules invariably leave the subjugated countries and communities badly divided and who would know this better than we Indians. It will be difficult to find a country that was under colonial rule to have remained politically and socially united within after the accursed regime lifted its shackles.

The World Imperialism of 19th and 20th centuries sowed the seeds of strife, acrimony, and animosity within the body-politic of subjugated nationalities, so much so that these traits have entered their DNA and keep resurfacing horizontally across the communities and vertically through generations. We continue to harvest the crops that are yielded as the embedded seeds are not lost in antiquity but lie in hibernation and breathe back to life through incubation and warmer climes provided by the international power-politics.

The world now knows the reality about WMDs through various sources, including American scholars themselves. More stories will keep coming out over the succeeding decades as it is happening today of the times of Lyndon Johnson, Nixon, Kissinger and so on. But meanwhile the world map would have irreversibly altered in some regions, considerably affecting the lives of millions of innocent people who unfortunately, in number, do not merit attention or compare to couple of body bags of the privileged ones. The worst indictment came from the Brazilian diplomat, Jose Mauricio Bustani as OPCW's Director General who should have been the best authority to establish the evidence of WMDs in Iraq and who denied such existence on the basis of his findings but was shunted out under pressure from USA. And the damage was done; we soon started learning new lingo such as 'smoking out', 'regime change' etc.

The war machines and ammunitions are anthropophagus. They survive on exporting and outsourcing deaths across poorer and weaker nations and claim human lives as fodder. According to Stockholm International Peace Research Institute study, America corners 30% of the global arms sales, followed by Russia 23%, Germany, France and UK together holding 22% (five nations, 75% share) and corporations eventually sell them. Whether it is a State or a Corporation, the cannibalistic traits have been endemic but they are not tried for war crimes. Might is right, as in ancient times, so also now, and the weak has no voice. While the world at large serenades on massive misinformation doses, leading to acquiescence and slumber induced by lullabies, it pushes the victims of such propaganda into deeper morass, with the last resort to Dark Age rectifuse – withdrawals, armed resistance, aggression, mindless violence and deaths.

'Chicken and egg story' like History repeats itself. The baying IS warriors out on the streets across the globe to give and take lives would be less in number and less lethal if greed of the super powers was capped and fairness and justice heeded by the international community.

Response in Difficult Times

It is unfortunate that the first column of the New Year from my pen should concern itself with terrorism abroad, rather than talking of things closer home or of something pertaining to our day to day life. But that is the need of the hour. What happened at the office of Charlie Hebdo in Paris was most reprehensible and tragic. It is also becoming increasingly unbearable to witness such wanton violence. Selective gruesomeness and killing of people for silencing dissent - yes, the right of literary and artistic freedom should be construed as exercising the right of dissent, or should we say defiance. When libertarians have given lives fighting autocracy and despotism, would they not continue to fight for their right to express their thoughts in any medium they like? How could these so-called 'Islamists' imagine that they would be able to wipe out dissent through violence.

If retaliation is not happening yet, one should be thankful to the core of the Western morality which is still overwhelmingly and conscientiously refusing to demonize members of a community, just because some fringe elements from that community have lost their head and taken recourse to a way that is not acceptable in the modern democratic life. But in the light of repeated attacks on their life styles in their own countries, how long will this equanimity last, is a moot question.

Dogmatic beliefs, narrow-mindedness, bigotry, prejudice against 'others', desire of vendetta and retribution etc. are the likely driving motive behind such attacks. The terrorists have decided to be the presiding judge and the biblical messenger to set things write. But what they are indulging in is the worst kind of crimes against humanity, and that too in the name of a religion that's name translates as peace. In the process, they are denigrating the name of Islam and causing irreversible harm to its adherents. Clearly their number must be very small. But the amount of mischief that they have been creating is many times more than their number and that is worrisome. They are pushing the Muslim community to the defensive, actually a precipice – protestations and exhortations of 'disownership' notwithstanding – the 'charge' has started sticking or would increasingly do if these attacks continue.

There are elements that keep a society together despite cultural, linguistic, economic diversities because there is also a shared consciousness that acts as the cementing bond. Even where this shared consciousness is missing owing to the presence of large number of immigrants, new settlements etc., there is important glue, namely, the rule of law. The Western hemisphere despite its avowed materialism and weakening family bonds, in comparison to the Indian scene, has definitely set for itself higher democratic principles, at least for their internal governance and they like to guard it enthusiastically. They attach high value to individualism, respect privacy and look down upon invasive social behaviour. The common people of France would be barely able to conceal their total bewilderment at what has been done to them for doing something as harmless as mocking somebody whom these perpetrators of the communal crime supposedly hold in esteem.

The dilemma is now very real and strong for a liberal Muslim. By the very definition of this classification, he/she would abhor and disown any acts of violence against another person, much less against a belief held or practiced. He feels worse when such violence is perpetrated in the name of the religion to which he also belongs. But if he protests loudly, would he be considered going against his own religion and whether he could afford to go that far? This dilemma needs to be resolved. At some level it is happening already. I noticed a placard that read, "If I am a Muslim, they are not, if they are Muslims, I am not". Perhaps Muslims can do even better but this graphic shows a way, i.e. total rejection of any violent creed in any part of the world from all those 'holier than thou' fanatics of the world, including the custodians of the sacred relic.

In the Indian context, despite various infirmities of our democratic existence, which in any case, apply to all communities, it has afforded members of every single community to rise in life and station on the basis of merit. Further, we have the constitutional safeguards against the abuse of power, the fiercely independent judiciary to enforce it, a very vigorous and free media, and most of all an exemplary civil society (coming from the 85% population of the country) that takes pride in taking a left of center position in all social, political and economic issues. A sitting MLA has been convicted in Gujarat and army officers court-martialed in J&K. So the system has the potential to deliver, even in most stressful circumstances. And where it fails, it fails for anybody and from any community. We keep saying metaphorically that poor don't get justice but that poor more often would be from the 85% section of the population. This fundamental understanding must down on the Muslims in India. They have to fight nothing but illiteracy and poverty. If the same is not being told to them by their Muslim leaders let ordinary 'non-leader' like you and I tell them.

Reason in the Age of Unreason

King Lear of Shakespeare lamented, *"I am a man more sinned against than sinning"*! Terrorists, including 'Islamists' or of whatever hue would perhaps be in this frame of mind while defending their stance of 'avenging the wrongs', purported to have been committed against 'their community'. They forget that they cannot stand the might of the modern state and would meet their nemesis sooner or later. Faced with the determined strength of the world and backed by global public revulsion against their misdeeds, their neurotic ambition has to end. So while we are concerned and even angry, worry should be limited to the apprehension of any further loss of human lives, but not about the eventual defeat of these misguided anarchists.

Our concern must also be about the deep fissures taking place in the global inter-cultural and inter-religious bonds that generally existed till recently. There is no doubt that sporadic terror attacks in the past and the recent mindless violence have been provocative. Keeping balance and composure in such a charged atmosphere is not easy. But that is precisely the test that Europe is called upon to handle today. The radicalization of a tiny section of Muslims, as asserted by the authorities in the wake of news of some of them joining ISIS etc. — hailing from the regions other than the zone of conflict— because an entirely different paradigm will apply on inhabitants of the conflict zone, is a matter of concern.

This trend, howsoever miniscule, perhaps in decimal percentage, must stop totally. It is ironical that while their family live in poverty and deprivation, some young fellows instead of struggling to improve their lot have chosen to follow the destructive utopian path presented by the ISIS and various assorted groups of 'Islamists'. Since the number of radicalized Muslim youth is very small and it is a new trend among them, their social reintegration would not be difficult. This needs thoughtful, deft and professional handling by the law enforcers and equally determined vigilance and support from families and the community at large.

Democracy provides processes for resolution of disputes through legitimate means, better if the misguided persons know this the easier way. The wisdom is not to play in the hands of agent provocateurs and not to fall for the diktat of the self-serving leaders — political or religious. A lead comes from the writings of Khaled Ahmed, political analyst and consulting editor of the Newsweek in Pakistan. Writing from a dangerous place, he constantly attacks the negative preaching and misguidance being spread by orthodox sections. In his recent article, 'The enemy within' in The Indian Express, he refers to the existence of 'supra-individuals' in Pakistan who highjack both the State and the non-State agencies. Clearly they would be doing this through manipulative and vitriolic campaigns carried out with the aid of demagogy and commandeering mesmerising hypnotic power. Khaled Ahmed categorises them as 'supra-individuals' — essentially creation of their own Government agencies; we need more courageous writers like him.

As for those cartoons, they are not as much satirical as often, nasty, offensive and insulting. Deliberate insult of others is neither creative nor the best literary expression. However, the opposition to or disagreement with any insult, ridicule or unfair criticism cannot be met by violence — the only option for a civilized world is rebuttal, counter-criticism or at best peaceful protest. This prudence, if not realism, must down on those who instigate, train and unleash some gullible young men from the community to the path of self-destruction.

The West has always prided itself about their openness, humanism, democracy, innovations, scientific discoveries and technological advancement that has catapulted them to such eminence vis-a-vis the rest of the world. Many modern social, economic and political institutions that we have today are gift from the West. Their modernism, therefore, should not be sullied now by surrendering to the jingoism of the fringe elements among them as that has been the trouble across the divide. It cannot be the turn of the democratic world to cause social breach. There is apparent need on the part of the civilized world to show continued restraint and responsibility.

Back home as well, there are of late some discordant voices aired regularly — divisive, venomous and disturbing. This cantankerous behaviour is sought to be matched by some lunatic fringe of Muslim leadership from UP and Hyderabad. Fortunately there is a strong body of liberals in the country from both the communities who do not subscribe to extremist declarations. We also hear and read several mature, sagacious, logical voices like Arundhati Roy, VasundharaSirnet, Shiv Visvanathan etc. from India and Noam Chomsky, Howard Zinn, David Harvey, David Brooks and several others abroad to name a few. The risky replication of divisive narrative by some in India must be guarded against. Equally the Muslim intelligentsia and the community at large must watch against leaders who try to take the mantle of 'supra-individuals'. Humanism and harmonious co-existence has to be the mantra, and the guiding principles by which material progress and freedom from the vicious cycle of ignorance and poverty can be obtained. If nothing else let enlightened self-interest and basic human intuitive intelligence guide all.

AFTERWORD

My association and friendship with Faizi Hashmi goes back a very long time, beginning decades ago when we were students at the Aligarh Muslim University, working to secure our Masters degrees in history. I recall that, even then, he impressed many with his lively mind and sharp observations on current affairs. His opinions were informed by an enviable breadth of reading, and oriented by an abiding concern to be useful to others, to make life better for his fellow-citizens. Perhaps that explains his choice of a career in the Indian Administrative Service rather than academia. He has held high office in various government departments, and discharged his responsibilities to great acclaim. But, throughout his long and distinguished career, he has never stopped thinking and reading, observing the realities around him, and sharing his thoughts with others through his writing. It is remarkable enough that he has sustained what amounts to a second career alongside a very demanding 'day-job'. Still more remarkable is that, while reflecting on the plight of masses of people in India, and measuring the everyday realities of their lives against the aspirations and shiny ideals that frame official policy, he has lost neither hope nor his good humour. His observations are sometimes acerbic, but his tone of voice is never sour. He remains as he was, all those years ago, concerned to be useful to his fellow-citizens, to convince them that they should, and that they can, do the right things to make India a better place for all of its people, and especially for the generations to come.

I welcome the opportunity to read his essays, thematically ordered and arranged in book-form. The spread of Faizi Hashmi's concerns is impressive; nothing is either too big or too small for him to take note of and comment upon. The smallest things matter – like the fact that in India people do not wait for others to get out of a lift or a bus before they push their way in. Such habits have a significant effect on quality of life, making it more stressful than it needs to be. Moreover, underlying these habits is a lack of interest in the dignity and upkeep of the public spaces that everyone, no matter how well off, must at some time pass through. That attitude explains why so many neighbourhoods in India's cities are spoiled by litter and foul waste, and on a scale impossible for the authorities to cope with. As Faizi says, people have forgotten how to care for what they hold in common. He does not accept that this attitude is explained by extremes of poverty or population pressure, the raw competition for survival or success. As he wryly observes, the well-heeled middle and upper class behave in just the same way as the poorest – except when they are abroad; only in India do they renounce the basic civilities without a second thought. So it is, as Faizi remarks with regret, that although India has been the cradle of many civilisations, boasts a striking number and quality of monuments, as well as a richly diverse geography and wildlife, it has a smaller tourist industry than tiny Singapore. And so also, more gravely, he notes, the wretchedly polluted state of India's rivers and waterways; and the absence of monuments commemorating the sacrifices of those who gave their lives to win India's freedom from colonial rule. If no-one living in India cares for India, for its present and its past, economic success will more likely aggravate than solve its problems in the future.

Of course, not all the realities Faizi observes are grim and depressing. Yet even the grimmest are relieved by his wit and learning, by his skill in calling to mind relevant 'wise words' from many traditions: we hear from Mark Twain as often as from Mahatma Gandhi. Penetrating historical insights and critical observations are interspersed with the sensitivity and empathy of a devoted civil servant. As one reads these essays, one becomes familiar with the author's voice, and the rhythm and quality of his attention. It is a personal delight for me to find that he is still, as he was so many years ago, such good company. His learning and caring humanity are precious resources with which to build hope for India.

Farhan Nizami
Prince of Wales Fellow, Magdalen College, Oxford
Director, Oxford Centre for Islamic Studies